Christ
CONSCIOUSNESS

SELF-MASTERY ORACLE

AMANDA ELLIS

ARTWORK BY
JANE DELAFORD TAYLOR

REDFeather™
MIND | BODY | SPIRIT

4880 Lower Valley Road, Atglen, PA 19310

Designed by Danielle D. Farmer
Cover design by Jack Chappell
Type set in Carol Etched/Academy Engraved LET/Agency FB

ISBN: 978-0-7643-6624-6
Printed in China
5 4 3 2

Published by REDFeather Mind, Body, Spirit
An imprint of Schiffer Publishing, Ltd.
4880 Lower Valley Road
Atglen, PA 19310
Phone: (610) 593-1777; Fax: (610) 593-2002
Email: Info@redfeathermbs.com
Web: www.redfeathermbs.com

For our complete selection of fine books on this and related subjects, please visit our website at www. redfeathermbs.com. You may also write for a free catalog.

REDFeather Mind, Body, Spirit's titles are available at special discounts for bulk purchases for sales promotions or premiums. Special editions, including personalized covers, corporate imprints, and excerpts, can be created in large quantities for special needs. For more information, contact the publisher.

We are always looking for people to write books on new and related subjects. If you have an idea for a book, please contact us at proposals@schifferbooks.com.

Other REDFeather Titles by the Author:
The Archangel Metatron Self-Mastery Oracle,
ISBN 978-0-7643-5713-8

Contents

Introduction 7

Working with This Deck 11

Preparing the Cards 12

Some Suggested Spreads 15

Introduction

Welcome to the *Christ Consciousness Self-Mastery Oracle* deck. This has been three years in the making, but also in many ways all my life so far. To explain what I believe Christ Consciousness to be, I think it will be helpful to understand some context and history of my journey: in a nutshell, how did I get here, and by implication, you also, if you are reading this. We all have many paths and experiences, and it is important to remember there is no right or wrong way to approach spirituality. Respect for all beliefs is paramount, as we all share much that is common, and learn from each other.

At the start of 2020 I became very aware of a gap in the oracle card market for a deck that would articulate so many of the beloved teachings of Jesus, but which wouldn't expect anyone reading it to belong to any institution, faith, or identity. Rather, I saw the tenants of Christ's teaching being applicable to anyone who wanted to live a heart-centered life, and to use the template He set to help us become Christed humans. The writings that follow honor all respective journeys but, it is hoped, give fresh perspective as to how to work with and aspire to live in Christ Consciousness.

MY JOURNEY TO CHRIST CONSCIOUSNESS

Back to where it all started. I grew up in a Christian home, was baptized and confirmed, went to a Christian school, and, as a family, went to church (Anglican) every Sunday. Throughout my upbringing, we went to many different types of church: High Church, with incense and ritual; Low Church, with less ornamentation and "fuss"; United Reformed; and Evangelical. My mum maintains the laying on of hands I had as a young girl healed a hip condition I was born with, which gave me bowlegs (long since gone). I would sit open-mouthed as I watched people dancing in the aisles and speaking in tongues. Unfortunately, I also saw the more extreme aspects of manipulated belief when a dear friend of my mother's sadly excommunicated us, after joining a religious commune where we were outcasts for being heathens!

As a child I enjoyed all aspects of church: the flowers and eggs at Easter, the summer fetes. I sang in the church choir with so many happy memories of the hymns, and special shows we would do, with *Joseph and His Amazing Technicolor Dream Coat* by Andrew Lloyd Webber and Tim Rice being one. We also sang one dedicated to Jonah, and annual nativity plays were of course also a highlight. My father ran Sunday school, and I recall my pride as he got us all belting out "Sing Hosanna," "Lord of the Dance," and other such tunes of the day! All while he thumped a tambourine, even though he didn't play any instrument officially. My father at one point also wanted to be a Christian minister and applied for training but was turned away. I recall the day the letter came, and a dark cloud came into our cottage, as though the church rejecting him zapped the joy out of his faith, and in hindsight maybe that seeded something in me too. Here was a good, honest, inspirational man not deemed the "right fit" for the church he had so happily served—what part of God denied him access and what part was man-made?!

We geographically moved around a bit after that and found it increasingly hard to find the right fit either; church became more of a routine and duty and less about that unbridled sense of belonging and happiness it had been earlier. As I got older, it was my choice whether to keep attending or not, and often I did, particularly on important dates, but my frequency lessened. There were times I sat and despaired at the dry teaching; I vividly recall the Sunday service a few days after the 7/7 bombings on the London Underground (where fifty-six people died), and the vicar didn't even mention it once—the whole country was in shock; how could it be ignored? I couldn't comprehend the lack of awareness, compassion, or ability to be able to deviate from the set script of the day because of the liturgical calendar. I left feeling even more depressed than when I had entered the building. It wasn't all negative though. I also recall a beautiful service at All Souls Church in London, where the minister gave an inspiring and very human speech about how we are all equal under God's eyes, and that if faced with someone who makes you feel inferior and unworthy, to imagine them naked or sitting on the toilet! Now this I could relate to; I could even smile and have a laugh—no dusty, hard-to-fathom dogma with little applicability to my life.

I think ever since that time (my twenties), I have been walking the Christ Consciousness path rather than the traditional Christian path . . . I am not against church, and you can still go to church and get great benefit from it, but for me my journey was now outside any building, place, set time, or, importantly, middleman or woman to tell me what Christ thought.

I left the church, but I never left Christ, and He also never left me. What instead presented was an opportunity to connect with Him deeper; form a close, loving connection; and be free to explore other beliefs and traditions without judgment or shame. Christ never left my side while I explored aspects of Buddhism, New Age, Hinduism, Sikhism—after all, why would He? There is no separation—that is a man-made construct—and everything under the sun is of God: multiple expressions, experiences, and an abundance of light, wisdom, and love to be found the world over.

I hope what this deck does is to deepen and widen your understanding of what Christ Consciousness is, which is a pure energy (supremely high frequency) to embody, hold, and be! I hope that it encourages you on days where it feels unobtainable, since we all falter; yet, to strive to do better, to operate from the highest frequency we can be, truly is Christ Light operating within you. Like a piece of heart-centered software, it becomes you. You ARE IT, and the instruction manual is laid via all of Christ's teachings of love, tolerance, humility, forgiveness, and more.

This deck was not intended as a straight run-through of every detail of Christ's life, nor a repetition of all that is said within the Gospels. Personally, I believe that in 2,000 years, the world has moved on (as intended, since God's creation was meant to evolve, not stay stagnant); the writings of the Gospels must be read through the lens of the times they were written in. Jesus today does not judge you (e.g., if you are divorced, are unmarried, or don't obey your partner), nor are you damned for exploring other aspects of spirituality—there is nothing wrong with accessing your true power and light. As children of God, we are meant to be curious! Jesus is on this journey with you and will take your hand to the degree you wish Him to. Respectful of all faiths, He works with all the other Ascended Masters too, wanting whatever helps bring you peace, healing, and in turn light to this planet.

Writing this deck and being involved with cocreating the ideas for each painting that Jane Delaford Taylor so brilliantly executed was to have been blessed with Christ's presence throughout. Initially I naively expected to sit down and write the words in one go, for the pen to move on its own accord, but of course what needed to happen was that I was asked to sit with each energy. At every juncture before writing the card's message, I would be presented with something in my own life to look at. Whom did I need to forgive? Where do I doubt or lack faith? Do I believe in miracles? Where am I still trapped (devil energy)? This is what Christ Consciousness gifts us, an opportunity to walk the path, explore, grow, and learn more about ourselves. Hence it wasn't rushed, and I do feel this is part of Jesus's gentle energy. We flow at our own pace, being asked to be present to all that unfurls moment to moment in God's time.

Throughout this deck the use of the names "Jesus" and "Christ" are used interchangeably; again, in traditional Christianity there is a difference, but to me these are both terms of endearment that I use in my connection with Him and are expressed not just as names but powerful languages of love and recognition. You may refer to Him in another way—Jeshua, Sananda, Emmanuel, Teacher—He responds to them all and will meet you in whatever way you wish to be met.

Please also note that references to God have the pronoun "He"' throughout. This is for clarity of writing, but I believe God to be both male and female, being all that ultimately is. Use of the words "Creator" and "Universe" are also sometimes used in place of "God," but again please refer to terminology that works for you.

The New English Bible and New International Version of the New Testament were used as reference points, and this deck also references *The Lion, the Witch & the Wardrobe* by C. S. Lewis and *The Wizard of Oz* by Lyman Frank Baum.

I hope this deck and book bring you into closer awareness of the Christ Consciousness within you, and that it is a valuable tool to access whenever you need support or guidance.

With all my love and best intentions on your forward journey.

—AMANDA

WORKING WITH THIS DECK

The fifty-five cards within this deck address many of the qualities that you are encouraged to work toward mastering if adopting a Christ Consciousness path. Some you will find harder than others, and day to day you can notice where your behavior and energy are aligned. However, do not judge or berate yourself for falling short of an idealized standard. The template Christ demonstrated so beautifully is a high bar to set your sights on, and you are a human being; it has taken humanity 2,000 years to get to where we are today, and yet we are on the brink of great breakthroughs in self-awareness and are always supported to do our best. Mastery is within reach if we believe it so, work toward it daily, and commit to a path of enlightenment, prioritizing what is important and honoring our own soul.

In the pages of this book, you will find references to Christ's teachings, questions, highlighted areas of suggested practice, and instructions to assist you while working with the cards. Above all, the practice of carefully studying and reflecting on the words and images will give you a chance to engage your higher self, to tune into both Jesus and yourself to find the answers you seek.

This deck is meant to challenge and inspire you, helping you live a fuller, authentic life, free from worry, doubt, and fear, while accessing your own divinity and light.

Although the cards may ask you to consider the past, present, and future, they are not designed to be used as a fortune-telling aid, but instead as empowerment tools and focus aids. We are all-powerful co-creators and master manifestors in control of our destinies and lives, whatever is happening around us.

The cards are also intended to be used as a healing tool, helping you understand underlying causes by offering insight from a higher spiritual perspective, and suggested solutions and support. You will be prompted to think about what each card brings up for you, whether it is something to work on or a gift to be received. The cards can be used both for personal readings and readings you do for others.

My hope is that you will be touched by Jesus's presence, feel His power behind you, and feel the Holy Spirit working through you as you work with this deck. May you enjoy using it as much as Jane and I enjoyed creating it!

—AMANDA

Preparing the Cards

FIRST TIME OPENING YOUR DECK

Hold the deck in your hands and feel into its energy, invoking the energy of Jesus and focusing on your own heart energy.

Breathe and ground your energy by feeling your feet on the floor, then also become aware of your crown chakra energy above your head gently opening. Affirm "I am ready to receive all blessings, instruction, and guidance—thank you, dear Jesus."

Then with your hand on your heart, allow it to gently open to the loving energy present and make a connection between your heart and the deck in your other hand, or on the table in front of you. Imagine a bridge of light flowing between your heart and the deck, and give thanks and gratitude for the gift and this present moment.

Say aloud (if desired):

I bless this deck with the energy of Christ and the highest light. May it be a beacon of strength and hope in times of struggle and may it also offer me growth in times of ease. May it be a bringer of new ways and ideas, and birth in me and all it touches the impetus to live in Christ Consciousness. Let it give me guidance when I am stuck, and motivation always to be the best version of myself, so that I can discover more of my divinity and see that in others also. Thank you. Amen.

This invocation can be used before each reading that you do going forward too.

Then spend time connecting briefly to each card. You may like to touch each one, noting its presence in the deck and your initial response to its image; some may attract you, while others may make you pause, reflect, etc.

Then gently shuffle the deck and place the cards facedown, ready for your first reading with them.

The deck is already protected from lower energies, being full of Christ's teaching. We should remember that just His name invokes safety and brings in His golden ray, which keeps all harm away. However, if you wish to also place rose quartz and clear quartz crystals on top of the deck (boxed or unboxed), it can further boost it, keeping it clear, so it is always ready to be used. It also strengthens your connection to the deck.

THE CARDS

The cards can be pulled intuitively, and you are encouraged to come up with your own spreads that work for you. The ones given below, ranging from straightforward spreads to more-complex ones, are simply suggestions to help you get started. Don't get too constricted when working with a spread; remember that the cards should be read intuitively. It is important to look at the overall feel of the cards selected and how they relate to each other. Also, take note of the messages you are drawn to and those you resist!

If you don't understand why a certain card has appeared or are confused by it, sit with the card for a moment and feel into its message. If you need further clarification, pull another card to go alongside it, and as you shuffle, let the cards know this is a card needed for clarification. In general, whether doing your own spread or one of those listed below, trust what gets pulled. Don't be tempted to pull again to receive a different outcome!

Also, treat the cards, and energy you are working with, with respect. You should not repeatedly ask the cards the same questions, since this shows a belief that you can't trust them or your own intuitive ability to read them. The cards will seldom be wrong!

Take note of cards that appear often when doing different spreads for yourself or reading for other people. A repeating card always needs to be fully acknowledged for what it is trying to teach, whether at collective or individual level.

Cards can be shuffled in any way that feels right for you. Selecting the cards can be done in different ways, too, either by fanning them out and choosing card by card, or by shuffling them and taking the top card and bottom card of the deck. Another way is to count them, pulling the number card you intuitively feel drawn to; for example, the fifth card from the top, the eighth card, and so on. There is no right or wrong way to shuffle the cards, choose the cards, or even interpret the cards! Sometimes the cards will confirm what you already know, and sometimes they will give new levels of information.

Reverse meanings are not given in this deck, and that was not the intention when the messages were written. But, of course, feel free to experiment; it is your deck!

SOME SUGGESTED SPREADS

SINGLE SPREAD—CARD OF THE DAY

Shuffle the deck while taking three deep breaths in and out. As you center yourself, ask to connect to Jesus and to receive one card with guidance for you currently, whatever He feels you need to hear right now. This will be the most important thing you need to consider.

When the card is pulled, feel into its message. You may also like to place the card on your desk or somewhere that you will see it throughout the day. You can also lie down and place it on your body to absorb its energy and message, or place it beside you while you sleep, also to allow the energy of the card to support you.

IN-DEPTH SOUL GUIDANCE SPREAD

Useful at key moments in life, at times of change, or when insight is needed regarding a situation. Shuffle and select seven cards. Feel into all the cards drawn and the overall message, as well as looking individually at

Card 1—Gifts and blessings (even if hidden)
Card 2—Past influences/issues
Card 3—Current life lesson: what you are currently experiencing / working through
Card 4—Current blocks and challenges
Card 5—Guidance for next steps and action: areas to focus on
Card 6—Future energies
Card 7—Message from Jesus

JESUS

FOLLOW MY LEAD

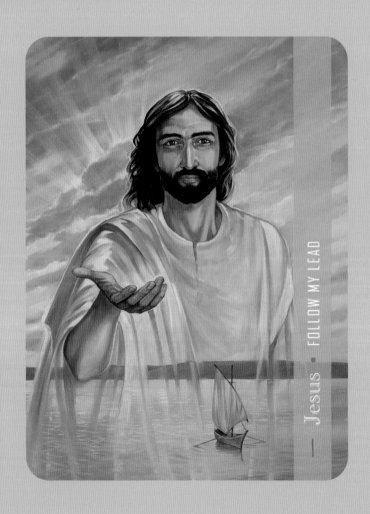

"Come and I will make you fishers of men," was Jesus's first call to his disciples. He calls again to us, this time knowing we understand more than we originally did 2,000 years ago, and that to be invited to hold His presence and embody His teachings is a lifeline that changes the game for all who answer it. This may not be the first lifetime you have walked with Him; you may have had an incarnation as an Essene, or another age where you may have been persecuted or been the persecutor for aligning to what man created wrongly in Jesus's name, be it war, crusades, material wealth in institutions, or other aspects. None of this was His desire or wish and was a distortion of all He stood for. His message was simply "to love one another as I have loved you," and now via the living flame of Christ Consciousness you receive another opportunity and time to pick up the mantle and follow His heart-led example, healing all that has gone before.

Coming to His energy now with fresh perspectives, you are not asked, however, to blindly follow, and not to question, debate, or bring your own experiences and learning to the table too. Jesus sees in you as He saw in the first disciples, Peter and Andrew, all your divine potential, and the impact you can make on this world. Not to push your views onto anyone, or to use belief as a mask, but rather to take up the challenge of what it is to walk through life demonstrating all He taught for your soul's evolution and growth.

If Mother Mary is the safe harbor to which you can return, Jesus is the boat and sail that drives you on; in His set template is all the "fuel" you require for the journey ahead. In times of smooth sailing and more-thunderous days, His light can steer, support, and guide you on.

Never mocking, scolding, harsh, or unavailable, His energy is always there day and night to walk beside you. Jesus is soft, compassionate, gentle, and wise and offers unconditional love, something we rarely experience in its fullest expression; it can reduce us to tears as it fills our heart with warmth to all. He asks that you try to live by the standards He set, to bring down the Christ Light to all who need it, by simply embodying it and shining your light. He understands your human frailty, the flaws that make us all imperfect, but loves you all the same, knowing you are doing the best you can, and seeing everything that has happened and the factors that make up the sum parts of your existence.

Your light and truth are not to be hidden in dusty old buildings, but out there on the street, in the shop corner, within families and relationships, and at your workplace. To be a living testimony to love, to help heal, illuminate, speak, and express it because you are it, and in His name, you truly remember that. Be confident; you are a beloved child of God, a spark of creation, a unique presence that this world needs to make it whole. He asks that you never deny your greatness, your own divinity, or all you came here to be; instead, to set the benchmark for others to follow, via your inner peace, radiance, stillness, tolerance, nonjudgment, and more.

Come take His hand and invite His spirit into your heart; here His energy dwells, seeding your own Christ Light, not looking outside oneself to find it, but bringing it home.

SISTERHOOD

THE FEMININE WAY

Sisterhood · THE FEMININE WAY

2

Sisterhood is highlighted, and you are asked to examine how women have both shaped you and made you who you are today. You may have been blessed with great nurturing, steerage, and love from a mother, friend, partner, colleague, or daughter; if so, take a moment to thank them now and honor the bond between you still. If you didn't have such a positive influence, call on Mother Mary and Mary Magdalene to guide and heal you and teach you feminine principles such as receptivity, sensitivity, patience, gentleness, and a new way forward.

Think about whether you value women's strengths, ways, and wisdom, in turn honoring their gifts. Are you a champion for women, helping support and build them up, or does part of you feel threatened, wanting to belittle or not be there for them, maybe, triggered by jealousy, gossip, or greed? Often such lower subconscious behavior stems from having never had someone to champion us, or feeling as though there is not enough love to go around, so we may fight over it. Do you have women in your workplace, family life, or peer group whom you battle with? If so, seek to bring in wisdom and peace to these relationships, and to yourself.

Women joining forces to change our world birth new paradigms. Historically, women uniting arrived via times of adversity in our world. In World War II, women had to join the workforce to keep the home fires burning, women also had to come together to secure the vote, and still in some countries, groups of women demand and campaign for education for their children as well as other basic rights.

To meet the deep division in our world, women need to come together again to help raise the flag for the Divine Feminine energies to bring in a softer, more caring world. Irrespective of gender, the feminine principle arising in us all births the New Age. We may struggle with knowing how to do this and where to start, but it is via simple daily actions that we change the world.

Both Mary Magdalene and Mother Mary would have worked together through Jesus's life to support His mission and bring in change; they would have shared confidences, tears, and joy. They held their own considerable light, which, when combined, was and still is a powerful force for good in the world. When looking into this picture, you will see the softness, gentleness, and grace they both held, the sense of companionship devoid of competition, distrust, or misunderstanding. Sitting basking not only in the majesty of God's creation and the galaxy above but in the appreciation of each other. Knowing they could each learn from the other as well as draw strength, comfort, and inspiration. They are able also to be in silence, present in the moment, knowing that the most powerful creative force of the universe was inside them. They invite you to join their sacred circle and to share stories and hopes for the future. They bring forth tales of ancient lands and times, legends, myths, and more, of women of history and your ancestral line too. There is all the time in the world to bond and deepen your connection with them and your own feminine energy. Allow the energy of true sisterhood to enrich you.

WISDOM BRINGER

EARTH SCHOOL

Much of life is a rerememebering of what we already know. We come into this incarnation from pure spirit, with eons of lifetimes of acquired soul knowledge. The journey back to remembering who we truly are, where we came from, and where we go back to is the biggest adventure of all.

When here, despite the great wisdom we have within us, it often lies buried waiting for the moment it is needed and can be retrieved. As children we enter education and learn what is on the curriculum, yet what is contained within us is far greater, with more depth and breadth than we can imagine. Our senses are our antennas: they can guide and steer us to learn to trust ourselves regarding "what feels right and what feels wrong" and "what appears to be true, but I sense is not." What sounds harmonious and what words and energy hurt my ears?

When you look in the mirror, what do you see? A human struggling with limited understanding or a wise old soul who is waiting to be acknowledged? It is said that the eyes are the doorway to the soul, and it is interesting that when newborn, our eyes take a few weeks to mature and for vision to be clear, as if we aren't quite ready for the veil to be totally lifted whence we came and to reveal everything. Stand tall today and see who you really are, a divine soul with lifetimes of experience where you have been tested and gained valuable firsthand knowledge regarding how to respond, react, and be. There is a whole library you can tap into to help you, a fountain of wisdom within.

Of course, acquiring new knowledge and wisdom never stops, and it may be that what you struggle with now is in fact your greatest teacher. The problem at hand is trying to lead you to the solution, and the difficult relationship may be there to teach you, including how not to be, or what not to put up with. There are opportunities to learn from every interaction and experience. Ask yourself, "What can I take from this? What did I learn today? What is this person trying to show me? Why am I finding this difficult?"

It may also be time to undertake some new study, from modern-day books to ancient texts and philosophical concepts. Indeed, the thirst for wisdom should never leave us; the desire to be challenged via debate, differences of opinion, and the sharing of knowledge is important.

The art of truly listening is also vital if we are to absorb and properly apply all that we learn. As such, we need to make proper time for that, space to process new ideas, and regular clearing out of what is unimportant (including what we hear; e.g., gossip and hearsay).

Look around today at what life really wishes to teach you; there is opportunity to do so from nature, travel, and meeting new people (even if it is a stranger on the bus), as well as going within to listen to our own well of knowledge.

Jesus also showed that what we need to learn may come from unexpected places. For example, the beggar having more to share of worth than the rich man, the child comprehending more than the adult, the enemy more to teach than an ally. We are all at Earth School and come to share what we know, which includes how we can learn together as one.

JOSEPH
FATHERING & RESPONSIBILITY

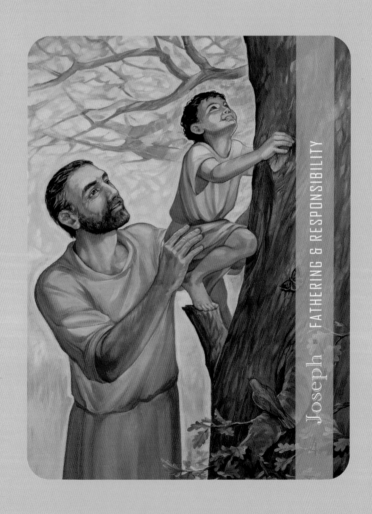

Joseph ▪ FATHERING & RESPONSIBILITY

Joseph reminds you of the soul contracts that you chose before incarnation, relationships you were meant to be in, tasks to do, work you were meant to fulfill, and how you were destined to serve God in many ways. It may now seem daunting, impossible, untenable, or even unfair, but you are reminded that everything in your life is a teacher and there to serve you in some way; you wouldn't have selected it otherwise, and you did select it at soul level. This may be through growth, finding skills, or qualities you never knew you had or deepening self-respect, or via challenge and proving endurance. Our mission and soul contracts can also be what bring a great sense of satisfaction and accomplishment as well as joy.

If we look at Joseph's story, here was a humble man asked to do an extraordinary job: to parent and raise Jesus, to watch Him grow, to educate and steer Him, and to ground Him in a family setting. Aware too of His greater heavenly father that Jesus answered to, but grateful and blessed to have been chosen for such an important earthly role. He served diligently, with no sense of his life having been derailed, instead realizing that the unexpected arrival of Jesus WAS his life's mission. As such, Joseph illustrates how to get to grips with life's twists and turns, the parts of the story that you can't see coming but need to face with grace when they arrive.

You are asked to reflect on the roles in your life, the soul contracts you have with particular people (that you may be conscious of or not); this can include family members, business partners, friends, and clients. Indeed, our soul mission contracts can feel like an uphill climb, a mountain that seems insurmountable; if so, call on Joseph for help. He offers practical guidance and spiritual support. You may be nudged toward a course, a person with the right skills to assist with, for example, childcare, house maintenance, or any aspect of daily life. Joseph offers solutions, and logic with a hands-on approach, to look at details, timescales, and resources, reminding you not to panic but to break tasks down into manageable chunks, taking time to methodically go through life with care, presence, and a steady footing.

In a digital age, he asks you to notice the trees, their branches reaching up to the sky, and their roots going down into the ground. To bear witness to nature, the changing seasons, and the animal kingdom too. The illustrated purple hairstreak butterfly is found in oak trees, and a whole colony can be supported by just one tree. They are seldom seen but spend their time in the lofty heights of the tallest branches, their symbolism being to soar but remain grounded, surrounded by kin and tribe.

THE MAGI
SIGNS & DIVINE TIMING

The Magi, or Three Wise Men from the East as they are also known, were among the first to recognize the energy of the Christed one about to be born. They followed the Star of Bethlehem, set against the midnight sky, to find and honor the light arriving, trusting that their inner and outer compass was correct and believing in the heaven-sent sign that Jesus was to incarnate, and their own intuitive feelings. They did not know where, and they did not know who He was yet, but they knew what He signified, the being who would leave a template from which Christ Consciousness would be laid for evermore.

They were highly likely to have been masters of astronomy and astrology and would have been waiting for such a divinely appointed time, knowing before others the significance of the moment.

Drawing this card may well signify that you too are receiving signs from spirit to follow your star, to walk toward your dream, destiny, and mission, indicating it is favorable to move, change, grow, and travel on. But maybe you doubt it or are unsure of the signs, even though divine timing may very well be here. This is a time to start to trust and act on the signs you receive, even if, like the Magi, others cannot see what you see. Learn instead to have faith in your own abilities, intuitive feelings, stirrings of your soul, and sense of premonition.

The Magi recommend you to be at one with nature, to start to read her cycles and behaviors, the way night follows day and the cloud formations and skies herald frost or storm or the peace of mellow days, and the heartbeat of Mother Earth. Knowing what is normal will reveal to you what is extraordinary: the unexpected snow, the welcome rain, the way Nature gives us signs all the time if we are in tune with her ways and heartbeat.

You have within you past lifetimes where you too looked to the sky and were able to tell the time from the sun's dial, the season from what was in bloom, or which birds were migrating. You are encouraged once more to divine into these latent skills, the knowingness you carry within your bloodline, which knows when to act and when to stand still.

It is also a sign that the Christ Consciousness light within you is growing, and as such you are given a purple robe of spirituality to deepen your learning and encouraging you to be the living embodiment of what you seek. It signifies it is the right time to heal and practice the tenants of what it means to be a Christed human; to demonstrate forgiveness, not to retaliate when another betrays you, to speak with peace, or to love your neighbor as yourself.

Jesus was gifted gold, frankincense, and myrrh to signify greatness in all these qualities to come. So too are you given these etheric gifts of frankincense for prayer and connection, gold for standing in your sovereignty, and myrrh for purification and release. The time is here to claim the life you were born to live, that which is destined in the stars and of which you are part. Follow your path and the light that will guide you to where you are meant to be at the perfect time. All is prepared and ready; your future awaits.

6

THOMAS
MIND TRAP & DOUBT

Thomas was the disciple who demanded proof from Jesus even as He stood before him as the "Risen Lord." How many times have we blocked the miracle or unexpected piece of good news because we fail to believe it can possibly be true? Old scripts and inner programming that "good things don't happen to me" or "I can't do it" run rampant and squash the magnificence of creation that is found in YOU and every potential moment. We can be cynical or afraid of being let down, unused to receiving, or just blind to the wonders all around us.

Too often we are driven not from our hearts but from the mind and ego, which want evidence before proceeding, yet the miracle zone lives outside the confines of what is possible or even probable.

In many ways Thomas was lucky; his declaration that he would believe only if he could touch Christ's wounds WAS granted. However, Thomas also showed acts of bravery and faith elsewhere that have largely been forgotten where no such confirmative sign was central to his decision-making. He was the disciple who traveled to Judea with Jesus despite fears for their personal safety. He showed courage there; so too his quite well-documented missionary work to India in years that followed . . . hardly the feat of a man consumed permanently by doubt and lower energies.

Thomas, like all of us, represents times we believe and gather our strength and courage, and other moments when our fear or doubt takes over. He represents being human in all our differing moments of weaknesses and strength.

Belief itself is seldom a static unmoving energy. It ebbs and flows like the sea; sometimes we will be granted signs (proof), answers to our prayers, and sometimes we will have to carry on regardless, feeling as though we are stumbling around in the dark. But God never leaves us. We may miss signs or reject them, but God never abandons us.

Having Thomas near you today is a sign that it is OK to be human. Maybe you are confused or in doubt; if so, be gentle with yourself. You may be questioning your ability to cope, to fulfill an obligation, or to meet a goal or task. You could also be going through a dark night of the soul, questioning everything and not knowing what to believe anymore. Truly, however, such moments serve you; they filter away what is no longer relevant and shine a light on what is. Sometimes this will tie into a crisis of faith, but it is not wrong to question; it is how we grow, and we are not intended to take everything at face value either. Balance is needed always.

These doubts may apply to any area of your life: to relationships, fighting an illness, your ability to find work, finding care for a loved one, having the patience to care for children or elderly relatives. We are tested in many ways, but we are never set up to fail; strength lies always within us, as does spiritual help encouraging us on.

Today it is OK to ask for a sign; it may come in unexpected ways, not as you imagine or request it. Be open to signs that confirm, but also realize that they don't always have to come. As with Thomas, he grew to realize he didn't always need one either; his heart already knew—it was his mind that bought the doubt, trapping him, but from which he also learned to break free.

PETER
DENIAL & WEAKNESS

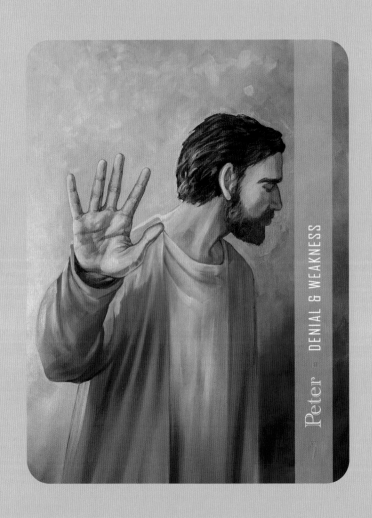

Denial; behavior we have all experienced, whether in our own life or someone else's. Pulling this card today may signify this shadow aspect is coming up for you now. Only you can know by going within what you are denying, since the expression of it can be varied and the reasons often subconscious or based on fear of what others may say, think, or do. We may be unaware we are in denial, with patterns so ingrained, to expect nothing or settle for less than we deserve; we are oblivious to what we miss out on.

We can deny ourselves kindness, healthy food, time to pause, healing, forgiveness, or an opportunity to begin again or to listen to our spirit. When in denial, deep within we know there is another way to be, something that needs acknowledging, doing, or changing, but we sit unable or unwilling to face it.

Very often we deny the one thing that we really need tied into feelings of fear, unworthiness, or not knowing how to access our own power and light.

How many times have you denied the magnificence of who you really are and what you can do? You have the answers, capabilities, and resources within you always. This card asks for reflection on the parts of yourself that are hidden or withheld from private and public view. You may have passionately held opinions and want to stand up and be counted, but you stay out of sight for fear of being singled out in public, on social media, or within relationships.

Peter, despite his deeply held views, denied Jesus three times; he was terrified, not wanting to be associated with the cause that would end up gladly being his life's work. By denying Christ, he denied his own light, wisdom, and journey that he had witnessed and been an integral part of. His actions were tied into "saving his own skin," putting his own ego and fear before his great heart and deeper knowing. By hoping he could hide and merge into the shadows, he sacrificed his own principles and beliefs. It was easier to follow the crowd than stand alone. We know Peter came to bitterly regret his actions, and his energy encourages you now to defend who and what you are, even in the face of ridicule, oppression, and misunderstanding.

Standing up for your mission, abilities, sexuality, beliefs, moral code, and ethics, anything that defines you as YOU, is always worth it. If we do not, like Peter, we live to rue our decisions and weaker moments.

Denial can also be a powerful teacher. However, by falling into its trap and learning from it, we often gain strength like Peter did to fight back, becoming stronger than ever and shining brighter. He is known as Peter the Rock, upon which the legacy of Jesus's teaching in the early church was built. Jesus was aware that Peter would falter, but stood back, knowing the experience would end up being the making of him. Sometimes we need moments such as these to help us grow, but by nature they should be transitory. Staying in denial for years is unhealthy and unwise; being true to who you are is vital. Reflect on the energy of the word "denial" today; see what it stirs within you and what it reveals, and ask for blocks to be lifted to see the way forward into the light once again.

8

HOLY SPIRIT

WORK THROUGH ME

Holy Spirit · WORK THROUGH ME

"Holy Spirit, work through me now" is about opening yourself to be an instrument for Love, Peace, and all that is good. When we take off the shackles of control, human ego, and doubt, we allow the spirit of higher consciousness to soar within us and in the world—rising from the flames of lower thought and deed to see the higher perspective and horizon, where there are always solutions, another way to look at something, or another method of work.

The Holy Spirit galvanizes your own divine self to respond from a place of grace, compassion, unity, and love. With this living energy within you, no small-minded human reaction or thought can persist as its love moves through any block or problem that requires healing, seating God's presence within the root of it. It also carries the miracle-zone energy, transcending all that is expected or likely into something incredible and unforeseen.

The Holy Spirit also touches our senses and how we interact with the world, what we can see, touch, taste, smell, and hear; we become the living lotus whose petals flutter and fragrantly perfume all those blessed to be near us, helping elevate consciousness breath by breath. By speaking in softness, joy, and elation, our words tumble like a waterfall—glossolalia in action, the spoken word of God running through you, birthing new dawns and new realities. For yes, the Holy Spirit is alive, always present, and ready when you are to receive and transmit its divine frequency, which may be now.

This card suggests that you may need instruction, support, and guidance, and that you may feel all paths are closed, the way forward unclear, the goals too hard, the energy stuck and futile. If so, receive the gift of the Holy Spirit; see it embodied as a dove above you wishing to anoint you with its blessing and seed its light within you today.

As the dove approaches, you hear it coo, you see its brilliant whiteness, and you feel its fluttering wings and the refreshing energy of freedom, faith, and flow that it brings. Sit and be with it as it lands on your chest, its beak gently tapping your heart center, opening the chambers and locked doors long held there. Permit the dove's energy to enter your heart, reassuring you of your place in the world, making the next part of your journey easier as you allow the divine to work through you now. For you are not separate from it, or it from you; the source of Love and Light is at one with you.

You can also call on the Holy Spirit to bring about truth and justice, to shine a light on what is unreasonable or unfair. You are never alone and, in every endeavor, can be an example of living Christ Consciousness, to do as Jesus would and shine your divine light into a world sorely in need of it.

Jesus knew that the gift of the Holy Spirit would be needed for times of persecution, struggle, turmoil, and tears; He knew also it wanted to sit within times of celebration and joyful praise and ecstasy. . . for God is in all moments, as are you, Father, Son, and Holy Spirit combined with your own unique essence, individuality, creed, color, or sex. Thank the Holy Spirit for being with you now, and go bravely into your day; all is well my child, all is well.

JESUS AND MARY MAGDALENE

SHARED MISSION

9 · Jesus and Mary Magdalene · SHARED MISSION

Our life's mission will often necessitate us treading new ground, which can make us feel vulnerable; it may require us to forge a new way, change a previous mindset, or create a new life, to go also against tried-and-trusted routes of old. To take the less trodden path rather than the familiar takes fortitude, courage, foresight, and vision, and you will be tested, but what is being asked of you will always be accompanied by support and guidance.

Your stamina will be required, and there may be moments of doubt and fear. But staying rooted to what you know you are capable of, as well as focused on the task at hand, will be a testament not just to your durability but God's alliance with you. We all need others in our life to help us carry our burdens and load. Spiritual assistance is guaranteed if you request it, but also reach out to people around you; seldom can we complete our missions and work without assistance from others.

Mary Magdalene, Jesus's closest trusted advisor and partner, came together with Him to combine their energy so He could lead thousands, generating strength from each other to fulfill the set destiny. Remember that whatever you face now, two heads are often better than one, and solutions arrive via taking advice and support from those closest to you. Try to include others in your plans and allow them to share your journey with you: the happy bits as well as hard places where you stumble and fall. Note those who are loyal and appreciate the role they play in your life. No man is an island, not even Jesus. He benefited from the kinship of His friends, family, and loved ones; He didn't push it away or feel above the warmth, companionship, and human touch offered. He also understood that to complete His mission allowed others to complete their soul contracts too, from Judas to Mary.

Mary, as trusted confident and the "one who knew Him best," was never far from His side, and her faithfulness and presence helped ground and root Jesus when He walked the earth. She also helped Him enjoy and see beauty in the whole human experience.

You are asked to think about whom in your life you can rely on, the service others have given to you, and to give thanks for all they have done. If you lack such support, ask Jesus and Mary to call in the help you need to help you now. Your companion and fellow path traveler can be varied; an animal, a human, an online group, a community, or the presence of a loved one passed over.

See too the geese overhead on this card and the symbolism they highlight, which is about taking turns to lead; when one gets weary, another takes that place, yet always flying together, just led by a different head. So, both learn to delegate and agree to take your turn helping others too! The power of teamwork is highlighted, including your earthly and off-planet soul tribe, Mother Earth, and the wider universe all pitching in to ensure success.

Take time today to focus and align yourself with your path ahead, who can walk with you and what you require for your next steps, calling that in knowing it will come.

10

THE GARDEN
RECEIVE & HEAL

The Garden · RECEIVE & HEAL

10

Beyond this moment, beyond this happening, beyond this breath lies a garden, a place where we have already built Christ Consciousness together. Here lives Peace, Unity, Harmony, Respect, and Freedom. Here too there is no warring, fighting, or belittling; here there is only Love. This place, God's Garden, is not barred to you; the doors are always open, and the entry is free to anyone, whoever they are and whatever they have done. All who sit here are forever changed by the living consciousness of light and the sanctity of all life, from the flower to the butterfly to the stars and moon and sky. This garden doesn't await you only at death; its gates are open to welcome you right now.

Come sit a while in the Holy Presence of universal wonder and angelic light. Surrender and allow all that is good into your heart, and take time to marvel at the majesty of all creation. You may come to this garden anytime you need healing, comfort, or companionship; times when you feel low, unloved, burdened, or alone. Here you are always welcomed as a valuable part of all that is. Time fades, heaviness disappears, and pain diminishes as you allow the love of Jesus and the culmination of all he taught to envelop you.

New Earth, the Golden Age, the times foretold and that were worth the wait. Breathe and feel yourself in God's Garden, hear the birdsong and the gentle sound of lapping waves, and smell the scent of the newly opened flowers, all there for you to savor and enjoy.

> If you feel lost—come.
> If you feel weary—come.
> If you feel uncertain and unclear—come.
> Whatever troubles you now can be aided by entering the Garden.

Breathe deeply into your body, say your name aloud or to yourself, then repeat three times. Visualize the moon at its fullest, cascading soft peach tones of color into the sky above, now lit up with stars just for you. Focus on a star, the one with your name on it; feel its brilliance and the sparkle that holds your unique soul energy within it. Sit and face the sea on warm, dry grass and be shown clarity, truth, and the way forward.

Right now, you have the attention of the whole kingdom; you can ask to receive what you need and give thanks for what you already have. It is also a place to come just for time-out, solitude, and the need to temporarily stop, since life is fast and society hard-wired to go faster. Here no such pressures exist.

Take in the colors and aromas, allow them to revive you, and experience the different energies that ride on the breeze . . . Beauty, Happiness, Health all are nectar for your soul. So too, if there is a particular part of embodying Christ Consciousness that you struggle with, you can ask for insight around your blocks or state of confusion. Here in God's Garden, every moment gives a chance to be reborn, your soul never growing tired, only curious to learn and explore more.

JUDAS
CATALYST & SOUL CONTRACT

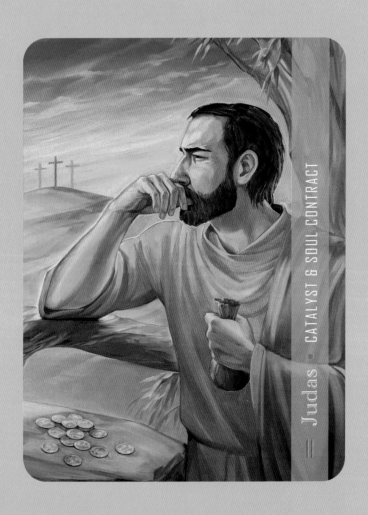

Judas = CATALYST & SOUL CONTRACT

Card 11 is a number associated with spiritual awakening (sometimes difficult), but for that to occur, we need souls or situations that are catalysts that lead us there; the partner who cheats so we learn self-worth, the redundancy that leads to a new career, the absent parent who teaches us independence, the disloyal friend who reveals who our real friends are, the illness that teaches us to make the most of every day.

This card highlights the soul contract of Judas Iscariot and asks us to see it was just as important as more historically loved characters whose roles were easier to praise and understand. Identifying who or what has played a Judas archetype in your own life teaches us much about ourselves and our contracts, as well as those who awaken and serve our growth through a more difficult role. Without Judas, there would have been no crucifixion, and without that, no rebirth.

Jesus truly understood that someone had to betray Him for His destiny to be fulfilled. He told Judas to do it quickly and, when kissed on the cheek by him and met by a crowd with staves and swords, admonished even His other disciples for using force to stop what needed to occur. Judas as emissary (someone sent on a special soul mission) deserves not vilification but love, appreciation, and understanding.

Picking this card today suggests there may be someone in your life, a situation, or an event that has deeply affected you. You may have been betrayed in some way, but as painful as such experiences are, they can rebirth us into something new. In time we look back and note we are who we are today because of them. We are given important opportunities to, for example, forgive, let go, and accept as well as find compassion for the one who acted cruelly. You may be going through this metamorphosis right now, and, if so, be gentle with yourself, since rebirth takes time.

Often only when we know another's story do we understand their behavior, how they were raised, what circumstances they lived through, their unhealed drivers and wants. If we look at Judas, he was driven by money; the thirty pieces of silver gave him no satisfaction, pleasure, or enjoyment. None of us like to be the one who is hated and vilified; we like to be the hero, yet you can't have one without the other. Both Judas and Jesus were tied into God's divine plan to show something far bigger, the resurrection energies that are carried within us all.

If we look at the card, we will see conflict and confusion on Judas's face because soul contracts are seldom easy when they arrive, and a veil of amnesia is often present where we forget what we signed up for preincarnation. However, if we can soften our stance to Judas and aspire to the forgiveness and respect that Jesus had for him ("Do what you have to do"), we can start to model that in our lives too. To see such "Judas" events or relationships as vehicles that deliver us from an old version of ourselves to the new and teach us much along the way.

TEMPTATION

MORAL COMPASS

Temptation - MORAL COMPASS

Temptation is defined as "the desire to do something wrong or unwise," and because this is highlighted by this card, caution is advised while counting to ten before considering one's next action or making an unwise choice. You may well have a situation around you that asks you to stop and reflect, as well as an opportunity to choose the higher pathway and consider what Christ would do.

Often, we are subconsciously driven by our lower natures and have relied upon programming and what we may have been taught or had done to us. Within this energy of Temptation sits Jesus's other teaching of "Do as You would be done by," for truly if that's our benchmark, we would never willingly hurt ourselves through word, thought, or deed, so we wouldn't wish to do it to another.

The Three Monkeys on this card depict the old proverb "See no evil, hear no evil, speak no evil"—with roots in Japanese culture, asking us to instead be of good mind, speech, and action.

In our daily lives we are bombarded by gossip, hearsay, and information that can often be driven by ego, agenda, and bias, not wisdom and discernment. Our job therefore is to filter out that which is misguided, unkind, or untrue and not be the receptacle that allows it to grow. What we say matters; our tongue should not be forked but infused with love. Take a moment to think about what is on the tip of your tongue: Is what you wish to say helpful and true, or spiteful and poisoned? If you face a difficult conversation, ask to speak with clarity, kindness, truth, and love, since even when it is difficult, if we speak from a place of love, it will be received as such.

Regarding our sight and focus, we are asked to turn our gaze away from unnecessary dramas, poor role modeling, humiliation of others, and any stimulus that results in lower energies within. We are not asked to be ignorant from the horrors of the world, however, and in fact the hands obscuring the monkeys' eyes are a nod to going within to seek the best way to help, maybe via prayer, power of positive manifestation, and focus. Jesus Himself never doubted that lower energies were prevalent in our world, and was tempted in the desert, but His focus lay in not giving it all-encompassing power, relying instead on God and rejecting false promises for short-term "gain."

Aligning to Christ Consciousness daily helps us hone our senses to act accordingly and to be a living example of how to live in thought, word, and deed, inspiring others as we do so.

Picking this card may also imply secrets and hidden motives are at play; someone may be hiding their true character or testing you. If so, see this as a teaching moment; to shine light on what is hidden; to help, not hinder; to forgive, not condemn. Others may be tempted in relation to earthly goods such as money, possessions, and power, but you can choose differently, knowing that the most lasting legacy is how you conducted yourself through trials and tribulations. Hold your head high; you hold the power to triumph over anything that seeks to diminish your beauty and light.

13

FORGIVENESS
SETS YOU FREE

One of the central teachings of Jesus was forgiveness as He knew it held within it the most powerful catalyst for positive change: freeing you and bringing in new possibilities and hope.

Pulling this card may imply there is someone or something you need to forgive; their deeds that hurt you may have been small or enormous, short or long term, and the damage to your physical, mental, and emotional health may be considerable. However, the act of forgiving is a process that can start today via a gesture, a thought, or simply a willingness to let go of the past. Forgiving is a present-tense action—it does not negate what may have happened previously, or pretend it didn't occur; it simply marks a line in the sand that from now on you will give less attention to what they did wrong and more to moving beyond it. Whatever has occurred does not define you; it is one part of a much-larger whole that makes up your multifaceted soul.

Forgiveness is card number 13 in this deck, and a nod to mastery, since it isn't easy or the first thing we think of doing when we are hurt; it can take time. However, as part of a path of healing it is vital, since not to do so hardens our heart; it keeps up our defenses and line of attack and can keep us in victimhood energy rather than the survivor who thrives. The 13th number always represents rebirth and what lies beyond the ashes of the old.

Forgiveness frees you, so today think about where you still feel tied to a past transgression, act of betrayal, violation, or unkind word or deed. It may be that you seek to understand another's motives—to see things from different perspectives or to learn something—or it might be unfathomable, but forgiveness is the same remedy that will help you now. We are not in control of how another behaves or acts, but we are able to control our own response to it. Over time, forgiveness will always come knocking, looking for the right moment to build bridges or simply allow you to let go with love.

This card shows former enemies across the barricades embracing as they recognize that by fighting each other, they are fighting their fellow brother. It shows that nothing is too big to be forgiven, and that much inner work will have preceded the embrace. Putting down arms is a gift not just to those involved but every generation that follows.

We are shown how Jesus acted when He forgave; a pertinent teaching was "Forgive them, Father, for they know not what they do," which seems especially relevant for these changing days where many are still blind to their own higher consciousness.

When we know better and have Christ's footsteps to follow, we are encouraged to be the one who holds the olive branch of healing out to another, knowing that we will be surrounded by spiritual help, light, and protection in doing so. The embrace of two souls who were lost to each other is greeted by a chorus of joy in heavenly realms, just as the cries that came before it are watched over and held too.

Forgiveness can also be an act we need to gift ourselves when we have been our own worst critic, driven ourselves too hard, abused ourselves, or not looked after our own needs. However, forgiveness figures for you right now. Tread softly with love and the deep wisdom within, and take a step toward it now.

14

GRACE
BLESSINGS & GOODWILL

Grace · BLESSINGS & GOODWILL

14

Grace is both a blessing and a gift that is offered to you now, to feel and experience God's love. It is given simply because He loves you, with no expectation other than to anoint you with it. In addition, this card also asks that as a divine being, you both hold and offer Grace, becoming a torch bearer that brings light to the darkness, both in yourself and others. This is mastery in action, and we can emulate the example of Jesus, noticing that all who were in His presence were graced by His gentleness, serenity, calmness, love, and peace. His proficiency in personifying grace stopped people in their tracks, made them change course, and made them want to be better human beings, turning away from ego and toward their divine spirit.

Managing your responsibilities and tasks with grace also elevates everyday life to be a display of God's work in action, affecting everyone you meet in interconnected ways. By doing so, you rise above the ordinary and ride the wave of the extraordinary, gliding with ease as the bee does in nature, knowing nectar is available in each flower and moment. The bee does God's work, creating both the honey, which brings sweetness to the table, and the pollination for our crops to flourish. Bees also teach us to be focused on the task at hand, their honeycomb structures a perfect symmetry showing what can be achieved when we work together in harmony with each other. An early reference point to the Christian church, bees also symbolized Christ's qualities, and beeswax candles became the soft light used in dwellings and places of worship.

Start to see whatever is in front of you not as a trap, test, or obstacle but an opportunity to personify grace, goodwill, and your alignment to a higher power. History has many examples of people facing trials, tribulations, and injustices, but their grace carried them through their darkest moments, since grace is a living energy that sustains and nourishes, both moving through you and becoming you.

God's grace is seen in so many things; take a moment today to truly witness and hold it: from being gracious in defeat, to being the point of calm in a queue of frustrated people, to helping someone who has not extended the same courtesy to you. Myriad moments make up a grace-filled landscape: a heartfelt smile, cheery wave, taking time to have a conversation with a lonely neighbor, the charitable act that you do not have to do . . . all of these are acts of grace and by their very nature elevate your own consciousness and in turn the planet's vibration.

Grace is gifted freely—it does not come with any condition or expectation for something in return, although the universe always notices and thanks you anyway. Thinking about your life, how could you demonstrate grace today? Is there an opportunity to give back to another, to give freely, to be of service by offering your grace and presence? Stepping into grace reminds us we are more than our lower thoughts and actions; we are God's creatures that are here to bring beauty and joy to our world.

Ask to be touched with God's grace; feel its energy as it touches the crown of your head and helps you be the highest version of yourself today. Smell the blossom in the air, feel the sun against your cheek, and see the wonder all around, for truly we are blessed to be here, and by grace our deeds are known as holders of Christ Consciousness.

THE HEART

WHAT WOULD LOVE DO?

"Love one another as I have loved you" was one of Jesus's last and most-important teachings and at the heart of Christ Consciousness living. So often we forget the premise of why we are here, or as Jesus said, "As my Father loved me, so I have loved you." We look at a world where aggression, division, and hate seem commonplace, but this can be countered with heart-centered consciousness if we drink and share from the chalice of love, remembering what life is truly about.

To be the fountain from which others can remember "What would Love do?" Not an easy task and very often not our first reaction when we have been wronged, misunderstood, chastised, or hurt, but in truth it is only love that will heal any wounds.

Love will help build the bridge you seek today, and it will help smooth any conversation that needs to be had. It will bring support, since love can never harm or be the wrong course of action.

Even if you have your loving gesture rejected, the fact that you offered it serves you and the wider world, since no drop of love is ever a wasted. A loving gesture, a kind word, a warm hug, a thoughtful gift or offer of your well-intentioned presence is never a mistake.

Into all karmic wounds love can pour, into all broken hearts love can soothe and bring relief, and into the bleakest days love brings the ray of light that transforms and makes life worth living again.

Remember today that your true nature is love, that you come from love and return to love, and that whatever troubles you have can be helped by opening to love.

So often we close our hearts because we have been hurt or expect little, but we also may not have received love as a child or may now be around those who are emotionally closed.

Like a clam, we keep our heart hidden behind an outer shell, but when we open it, we find the pearl within, not damaged by adversity but strengthened and polished via its experiences. Because to keep your heart open despite anything that may occur is central to Jesus's template; His love never faltered, and He knew it was and still is the most powerful force in the universe.

Receive today all the love that you require. Let it replenish you, inspire you, and fill every cell of your body with its magic and creative power. There is a never-ending supply, enough to go around, and it flows daily to you upon waking and on retiring to bed.

Wrap those you worry about in love; see it as the living energy that it is; send it also to your family, friends, and colleagues, as well as to those who trigger you, those who are jealous of you, and all perceived enemies too.

See love going before you as a stream of consciousness into the future. Feel it within you right now in this present moment and celebrate the love behind you as you heal your past. Love changes the frequency of your ancestors and those who have gone before, as well as those still to come and those still present.

Love is all there is, and all there ever will be. Bathe in its frequency today and drink from its cup, knowing that the well never runs dry, and many hearts are awakening more, as is yours.

16

NONJUDGMENT
REFLECTION &
PROJECTION

You are reminded how quick our human response is to judge others, and how fast we can also be judged, not by God but by our fellow brothers and sisters. So often this is done from a moment of rashness and haste, ill-thought-out words, intentions, and actions that cause unnecessary pain and suffering and that we often live to regret. It can be amplified by the pull of a crowd, or a groundswell of popular opinion online that creates a movement to attack and seek revenge rather than to listen and create a space for healing.

However, when we judge another, we fail to see the times we have acted without thought for someone; when we have done wrong or had malice, selfishness, or anger within our heart. To be human is to err, and no person alive has not done something misguided, unwise, or unkind. Our misdeeds may be large or minor, but all of us have a weight we carry that represents the times we did not hold true to Christ's teaching of love and nonjudgment.

We can blame, criticize, or attack one another for something we have done or, via an alternative life path, might have done. We also project onto others what we do not wish to acknowledge within ourselves. Whatever is highlighted, Jesus never demonstrated condemning another; He always offered the olive branch and opportunity for healing. In His own words, "Those without wrongdoing cast the first stone." For He knew it was not for us to judge, and that hate leads to more hate, war leads to more war, and judgment leads to more division.

Practicing nonjudgment is one of the hardest parts of Christ Consciousness but also one of the most rewarding to try to master. It is OK not to succeed, as you will, but we all learn from times we fail, and the lesson is to strive to do better next time.

Judgment and condemnation lead to a vicious cycle of increasing isolation and separation. Our human instinct to pick up the stone is there from earliest imprinted times, but so too is the template of a more Eden-like energy that saw all in God's Garden "as good." In truth, within everything is a spark of goodness and light; nonjudgment seeks to remind you to focus on that rather than the darkness.

Jesus also taught to love the wrongdoer (sinner) but not the wrong (sin); in this He showed us that we are all greater than any deed. That what lives within everyone is holy and far more than the sum of anything done in any one life, and that "your Father in heaven" loves you. That we are all part of a greater consciousness, and the angel's wing on this card shows the times a higher power, including your own higher self, steps in to try to thwart lower desires that want (e.g., vengeance, retribution), or to take out inner unhealed anger on another.

Reflect on what you judge: it may be behaviors in others; it does not have to be some big terrible deed. It could be intolerance, greed, egotism, selfishness, laziness, narrow-mindedness, or any other human trait. What we dislike in another is often what is reflected to some degree within us. Once identified, do not judge yourself; instead look at why the aspect is there. Where are their roots, and, importantly, are you ready to let them go? Seeing your human frailties and loving them back to harmony via softness and compassion is suggested. No battles of war, but the gentle embrace of nonjudgment and love is far more fruitful now.

LOVE THY NEIGHBOR

BEING OF SERVICE

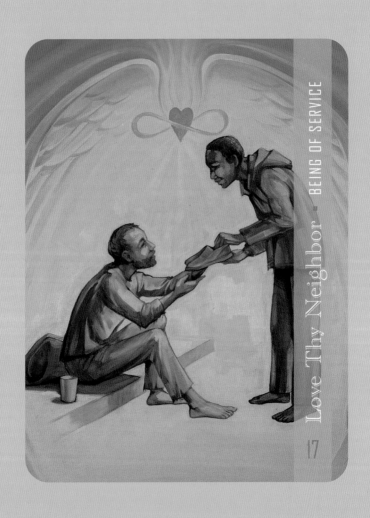

To be there for each other, to see every person as a member of the soul tribe, is one of the highest expressions of Christ Consciousness. Every day we can choose not to be the one to walk on by, but to do our bit to alleviate suffering. We cannot solve all the world's problems, of course, and we are not supposed to become burdened by them, but simply to do what we can when we notice and are able to.

It can be in the simplest act and does not have to be about giving anything more than our attention or presence. Stopping to smile at, acknowledge, and talk with a homeless person is just as important as the aspect of giving something material. "There but for the grace of God go I" is a useful adage to remember. We can all through a separate set of circumstances be the person who has lost their job, be in pain, be the outcast, or be the penniless addict. To see within the soul of one who suffers is an opportunity to show love and is what is important. Not to shun or turn away, but to be the one who asks, "How may I serve you?" Knowing too that what you give and do through each interaction serves you also. To see in the beggar, the refugee, the beaten woman a chance to be like Jesus and do as He would. And to exhibit the same care for yourself also.

Living in a world where so many have so much but where others have so little is a great imbalance. It may be that you are asked to stop and give thanks for the warm home, fresh water, safety, and comfort that you have around you now. Conversely, it may also be that it is you who seeks another's kindness, having fallen on tough times, not knowing how to cope or what to do. You may need words of encouragement, whether from a stranger in the street or a dear friend who knows you well.

Human need comes in so many forms; it may be mental, physical, practical, or all three, but where there is need there is an opportunity to do good for our fellow neighbor and be there for each other. For no one is an island, we all need each other, and it is important to remember that many find it hard to ask for help. This may also be true for you.

Being on the lookout for those in need of assistance is God's love in action, from those helping in community centers to simple acts of kindness that show you value the one in front of you.

Buying the meal for someone who is hungry, sitting with the child alone and ostracized at school, noticing the old person alone every day, or visiting the grieving friend. If it is you who are in need, be open and ask for help, anticipating that good people will respond, and not being too proud to accept charity or their support and aid.

In addition, you are thanked for the times you have been generous in thought, word, and deed. The prayers offered, the effort you put into helping another. It may be also that this card is encouraging you in charitable efforts, working for a humanitarian organization, providing meals to the elderly, donating to a worthy cause.

Every done deed is noticed, and every gesture and act of assistance is needed in a world crying out for love. You are thanked for all you give, and how you serve and all that you are.

18

FELLOWSHIP
SHARING &
COMING TOGETHER

Fellowship ▪ SHARING & COMING TOGETHER

18

This card depicts the Sikh Langar (free kitchen), a practice that honors unity and all invited (none denied) to food and nourishment. Prepared meals by volunteers are given freely to anyone regardless of economic status, caste, religion, gender, or ethnicity; all are seated together in fellowship, deserving of what is offered. It is said to be an honor to help run the Langar, and it is an integral part of the Sikh faith; at the heart of its practice of fellowship, service, and generosity is one we can model in our lives too, from cooking a meal for friends to those we do not know.

Fellowship in our day-to-day life is needed now more than ever. You may work from home, be a stay-at-home parent, live away from family, be retired and alone, or feel in some other way isolated from human companionship. Likewise, living in busy cities surrounded by people who feel like strangers can also be hard. The answer to both is to participate in a community initiative, to be with like-minded people and to share stories as you travel through your life.

You are a valued member of society, and your gifts and aspects that make you unique are precious and needed. It may well be that you already participate in community activities, whether leading them or simply enjoying them. The need to seek out others, to have human connection, and to be part of a group is healthy for you now. By sitting with others, we learn, grow, and raise our vibration as the energy of a group with good intent and love within their hearts amplifies and touches all who are present.

Are you currently feeling as though you are part of something far greater but somehow are on the outside looking in? You are encouraged to find fellowship with others, to call in your soul tribe, whether online or in person, and not to block messages or invitations to participate and enter the spirit of community. If you are nervous or afraid, ask Jesus to walk with you, to find new friends, acquaintances, and people you can enjoy spending time with. Fellowship is a safe space that can nourish you; here you find people who will be there for you, and with whom you can relax.

If you work in a competitive field, fellowship can remind you of the equal playing field and to slow down and enjoy the journey. In addition, fellowship can spur you on and motivate and encourage you toward a goal or ambition (e.g., to get fit, to complete a sporting challenge). You may also seek fellow souls as you go through a rite of passage, needing to share time with those who are new parents, graduating college, or dealing with widowhood, addiction therapy, puberty, menopause, and more!

An important part of fellowship is what you bring to the table, what you can offer and contribute, and the problems that you have worked through; the solutions you found are invaluable life experience to someone else. You may be thinking of starting up an online blog or creating an online community that can share news, positive stories, and more.

Primarily finding fellowship is highlighted today as a means for giving you renewed strength, passion, purpose, and inspiration; also, when heightening the power of combined intention of "when two or more are gathered in my name," extraordinary breakthroughs are possible.

PRAYER
CONTEMPLATION & CONNECTION

Prayer ■ CONTEMPLATION & CONNECTION

When you have doubts and worries, pray. When you wish to express gratitude, pray. When you need strength, pray.

Prayer is therapeutic for you now and can be done in any moment, in any place, when alone, or when with company. To sit and commune with a higher power, the universe, or your guides and helpers, it puts things back into perspective and helps balance your mind, body, and soul. Setting time aside to pray connects you with all the help you require, the energy to sustain you, and the solace and comfort you seek.

To pray is not to demand answers and solutions or to seek what you alone want, but to surrender to the flow of the universe, which knows what is best for you and all concerned.

There is often a divine timing at play with prayer, but our cries for help are always heard and answered in ways we often don't recognize. Just knowing that you are heard is powerful and cathartic, opening doorways to healing and peace.

To be in prayer is to be present, to pause, and to be still, allowing the outside world to recede and the inner one to grow.

Maybe you have been very busy or have not had time for yourself or your spiritual needs, since modern life is often frantic, noisy, and fast paced. But prayer slows down vibration so that focus, healing, and balance can be restored.

There is nothing too small or large that you can't offer up to God; anything that requires illumination and light can be prayed over. Prayer is never wasted time but is essential for greater clarity, faith, and endurance. Prayer can take us into a meditative state, changing our neural pathways in the brain and enhancing our empathy and understanding. It has both physical and spiritual effects that are long reaching.

Prayer will also help you reflect upon where you are at on your spiritual journey and what parts of the journey are a struggle and require help. It shows our commitment to evolving and learning and growing. Like a seed without water, a person without prayer will find it hard to thrive. Prayer puts you in touch with the energy you seek for whatever you now face. We know Jesus instructed His followers to meaningful prayer, and not prayer for the sake of being seen to do so either. He alluded to the private nature of prayer and laid down the Lord's Prayer as a teaching template, which encompasses giving thanks, asking for forgiveness, putting trust and faith in a higher power, and keeping lower energies and temptation away.

Prayer is not meant to be difficult. The child in this card has mastered it, knowing instinctively how to do it even against a city backdrop. There is a nod to the tranquility that can be found in nature also: a park, garden, stream, or tree; anything living that connects us to the power and beauty that is God's creation all around us. We don't need an ornate building to pray in, we just need ourselves and a moment to pause, breathe, and practice the art of communing with what we seek. In silence or via spoken word, prayer is a lifesaver and life sustainer. Enjoy a moment in it today.

20

ANKH

KEY TO LIFE

Ankh · KEY TO LIFE

20

The ankh as a symbol is given to you today, a blessing that has been handed down over thousands of years to those who seek to understand its initiatory power and meaning. Today it falls into your hands, and you are asked to carry its energy with you, reminding you of the sacredness of life in this world and the one to come. Find time to stop and reflect on the gift of your eternal life, appreciating the soul's passage through many lifetimes, dimensions, and portals. When we do so, we can appreciate that what we experience is always an instrument to teach and garner wisdom and learning, the soul never wanting to stop evolving.

The ankh's origins are heavily debated but are seen in many ancient civilizations, including Greece, Africa, and Egypt. In ancient Egypt it is seen in hieroglyphics, where it represented "Life" or the "Breath of Life." In this ancient society, an ankh was often depicted in the hands of pharaohs, gods, and goddesses and in tombs and burial sites to represent eternal life and safe passage onward. We see it held by the sun god Ra as a symbol of Creation, and also by the god Osiris and the goddess Isis, their union of male and female represented by the loop and cross said to bestow fertility upon Egypt, granting the waters, which is why it is also called "the Key of the Nile." In early Christianity it is said to predate the cross and was used by the Egyptian Coptic Church to represent eternal life through Christ.

Now with our deepening connection to Christ Consciousness, it takes on new meaning, reminding us of our soul's immortality and our connection to our own divinity. Not just for kings or queens and those in high authority, but for everyone as a reminder of the creator and the living consciousness of Christ within. The ankh unlocks your magnificence, your birthright, and your respect for everything that you encounter, as you recognize that just as you are God in a body, so is everything else (even if you can't see it). A multitude of different expressions of God having the experience of what it is to be human within a body. This card and this symbol are your key to see each new day as an opportunity to transcend lower limitations, knowing that this time matters, you matter, that God is in control, and that you are part of that God light.

You also see life as the precious gift that it is, just one page in a huge book that makes up your journey through many incarnations. You are reminded not to get stuck on one page or a particular period or problem; as with nature, seasons will change. You can let go just as the tree sheds its leaves, but you will always rebirth anew with fresh blossom and new sap.

The ankh also comes to you as a symbol of balance, for your masculine and feminine energy and your earthly physical life, and your connection to Higher Realms. To stretch out your arms to life as the ankh stretches out, embracing all it can taste, see, and touch and having deep roots that ground and an open expansiveness to all that there is. The ankh also offers protection in keeping you safe, knowing that nothing can damage a divine soul; all parts of you are intact and whole, all held in golden light and always reflecting the best of who and what you are, which is a shining light here to brighten this world and beyond.

GETHSEMANE

DARKEST HOUR,
STRENGTH ARRIVES

Gethsemane · DARKEST HOUR, STRENGTH ARRIVES

21

There are times in life, and this may be one of them, when what we are faced with and must endure can be very hard to bear. We may think we don't have the strength or ability to do what is being asked of us, and that we wish for whatever troubles us to be taken away, the problem removed, the obstacle eradicated, to go back to a more carefree time.

And yet, from a soul perspective, everything that we encounter in life is there to serve us, including the darkest periods. Yet, it is very human to feel scared, discouraged, and full of doubt and dread when we hit substantial problems or troubles. It is hard to foresee where walking the current path may lead and whether we will triumph. Our ego and fear can play mind games focusing on traps and worst-case scenarios, when really, we are asked to surrender and have faith.

Jesus in His hour of greatest need asked for the cup of suffering to be taken away from Him, tormented by what was to come but with the comprehension that this would occur only "if it be Thy Will not My Will." In that statement He showed understanding that a power larger than Himself in that moment knew the right course of action, for many reasons yet to play out.

So often when trauma and challenge occur, it can be the very spur that leads you on to champion something that is often far greater than just you. The person who finds themselves homeless one day becomes the spokesperson of the homeless; the bereaved parent whose child is killed by a drunk driver campaigns for changes in the law. The illness endured teaches much at soul level, whether it be resilience, courage, patience, etc. It can also be teaching those around you (e.g., to step into greater compassion, to be the prompt to mend bridges, to allow others the opportunity to give). There is always a higher plan to everything, and no experience is ever wasted at soul level. It is often through adversity that we find out how strong we are. This may be in picking up the pieces after an old life falls away; it can be role modeling to others to show them how to act and behave; it can be via simply showing to yourself that you can keep on going day in and day out.

Another important aspect of this card's teaching is that like Jesus, you will be given whatever it is that you need now to proceed, spiritual support is available, and you are not abandoned and alone. The gospels tell how an angel appeared before Jesus at Gethsemane as He prayed, encouraging Him on and helping Him recommit to His mission. This reminds you to ask for help, and that support will come but is answered fastest via a surrendered state. You too may feel an angelic presence around you as you regroup, pray, and pause at this time.

We see lying beside the tree a simple sword to help cut away doubt and fear and be the blade of clarity and light that shows the way forward; the slumped figure simply needs to stand and reach for it.

The cup (our predicament) shining brightly has a fated energy to it. Like Jesus, we may ask for it to be taken away from us, but it will command our attention till we drink from and tackle it. The ivy growing around reflects that the issue may have been present for a while, but that facing it will lead to greater spiritual maturity and strength. Do not fear it; walk toward it with faith.

22

PILGRIMAGE
ONWARD STEPS

The illustration on this card is based on the Pilgrim Steps at St Michael's Mount in Cornwall, England—a medieval path, and one climbed by those long ago who sought spiritual nourishment and enlightenment. In days of old they would have been climbing to visit the church at the top. While there is nothing wrong in doing this, today's pilgrim is often aware that the true connection to Christ is via the heart, and no building is required.

We still climb, though, ever upward, seeking connection and increased peace, presence, and awareness. Each step, some smooth and easy and others more slippery to navigate, reminds us that our spiritual path is made up of many events, people, places, thoughts, and energy. Some we relish encountering and others we would prefer to avoid, but all are necessary to navigate if we want to reach our destination. The journey from birth back up the Tree of Life, toward our eventual return to pure consciousness, is varied and takes unexpected turns. But as long as we keep our eye on our goal, we never will stay stuck and lethargic in the same place for long. We will see there is always a new vista as we move on to higher ground, while bearing witness to each place we stop at on the way, to reflect and take in the view.

You are encouraged to look back at how far you have already come, and how much hard work, dedication, and commitment brought you to the steps in the first place. You signed up for this life and came here to keep learning, growing, and striving to go higher. There is, however, no rush to get to the "summit"; rather, it is all about the journey itself, savoring each moment and taking in the day and night, the cycles of nature, and your growing development. Remembering what you once were and who and what you know now, acknowledging all achievements and not comparing progress to others but honoring your unique journey.

Pulling this card may also indicate that you are thinking of taking a pilgrimage; this may be formal, to a known destination, or to an informal, unmapped one. Pilgrimage is about going within, testing your own resolve, and exploring different ways of looking at the world. It may arise out of curiosity or necessity; you may feel burned out, needing time away from normal settings to realign and refresh body, mind, and soul.

The pull of a simpler life, a more stripped-back routine, may also be attractive, with less time distracted by technology and endless things to do. The calling may also be connected to letting go of some material possessions, identities, or an old life.

Often, pilgrimage beckons when we are on the apex of a new life; we are tired and wish to rebirth ourselves and find out more about what drives us and what we could be.

Taking time today to just stop and pause will serve you well, to notice and appreciate where you are at, knowing that in this moment you are learning something important. You may also like to sketch, draw, or think about where you would like to go, to future far-off lands or somewhere near today. A silent retreat, a walk in the valley or woods; anything is possible, as well as an inner pilgrimage via meditation, breathwork, or shamanic journeying. Enjoy the next steps and experiences as you learn more about who you really are.

23

RELIEVING SUFFERING

MOVE BEYOND PAIN

Relieving Suffering · MOVE BEYOND PAIN

23

You are asked to examine what you have been carrying (maybe alone) that has become so heavy it weighs you down. Like the cross on Jesus's back, it is causing pressure, stress, and discomfort, creating no peace of mind or ability to fully cope. You may have considerable baggage and unhealed trauma or pent-up rage or sadness. It may have been a long road you have walked, fraught with effort, hard work, and pain, or a shorter experience, but either way your energy levels may be low, depleted, and needing a period of rest. Considerable responsibilities and duties, whether from a job, your family, or just modern-day life, may be factors. Health may also be highlighted, whether physical, mental, or spiritual. A period of struggle you have gone through can certainly be indicated via this card.

The cross has long been associated with Jesus's greatest struggle but also His greatest triumph. You are reminded that you too will triumph over any obstacle you face, and that whatever has occurred is witnessed by spirit; the times you were isolated, alone, afraid, and in pain have all been part of your journey but will not be the end of you. Far from it, you will grow from what you have endured or are going through. Any deeply etched line upon the brow, any gray hair, shows the markings of one who has survived what would have vanquished lesser beings. You are both a fighter and a winner, an indomitable soul. Nothing is lost, just as nothing was lost for Jesus upon the cross. For He did not die but was rebirthed anew; the suffering was the doorway to something far greater, and every tear and anguished cry forged deeper wisdom, understanding of the human spirit, and faith in a greater power. "Into your hands I commend my spirit" were not the words of a beaten man or victim, but one who surrendered knowing that He would always be looked after even in His hour of greatest need. He never lost His faith, and neither shall you. You will never be abandoned, and truly at our time of greatest need is when we often feel closest to God's presence. You are assured that you will always be held, and God has a plan for you that may not be visible or obvious but is very real and present, and unfolding now.

You are asked to gently begin the process of releasing the old, stained shroud you wear; it bears the markings of what you were, not who you will become. A new gown awaits that is golden and illuminated with light. The shroud discarded on the cross reminds us that like Jesus, we are eternal beings given new keys to further doorways of existence and soul growth.

The poppies of peace mix with the poppies of suffering, old and new energies symbolizing that we never forget what we have lived through, but we can begin to make peace with it, realizing our life is the sum of many parts, light and shade, happy and tragic times.

Your story does not end here; it moves on, and all that you have learned will be invaluable wisdom to share. Your increased empathy and understanding will help many who have not "walked in your shoes" and fail to understand.

Taking your hand now, Jesus walks with you away from the cross to pastures new, filled with buttercup flowers and birds, where you are invited to give thanks to all that shaped you into the strong and valuable member of planet Earth who is precious and loved—and always was.

24

MIRACLES
MANIFEST & BELIEVE

Miracles · MANIFEST & BELIEVE

24

Miracles are possible in any moment if you believe. Picking this card asks you to have confidence that solutions and answers can arrive even if they feel elusive right now. You may be experiencing a degree of lack or shortage; it may be financial, around resources, success, romance, or any other area where it feels like an uphill battle. However, do not give up—you can win! Believe in the impossible and ask for help.

The feeding of the 5,000 is one of Jesus's most well-known miracles, turning five loafs and two fish into enough for everyone, with twelve baskets left over full to the brim.

You are reminded that this is a bountiful world with enough for everyone; the secret is to trust and share abundance with each other.

You may be encouraged toward acts of philanthropy right now, helping in your community, giving of your time and energy and experience. If so, whatever given will be returned to you tenfold, your generosity rewarded for helping others.

You may also feel as though you need others to help you and a miracle in your own life—doors may be closed to you, paths blocked—and you may feel as though you have no way out. But believing that a miracle is always around the corner will serve you well now.

This is not far-fetched, ungrounded fantasy but a firm belief in the goodness and magic within the very structure of this universe. To see the rainbow after a storm is a miracle, as are the first-born lambs in the field and the ducklings taking their first swim. When we truly stop and notice the miracles that are freely all around us every day, we pave the way for more to appear, as what we give thanks for grows. At the heart of the miracle zone, energy is gratitude that seeds the miracle to be born.

Jesus, when presented with the huge crowd and only minimal supplies, didn't panic or worry. Instead, He blessed what He had and gave thanks, and from that perspective and act, the miracle came. So too, when we see great need in our world and one person donates, it can create a large movement of others doing the same. It takes just one act of faith and the willingness to believe something is possible, knowing that a miracle's effect is far reaching, touching many as its grace ripples out far and wide.

The crux of the miracle zone is that action needs to be taken before you gain proof of what could materialize. In our own lives, when we, for example, start a business, face an illness, or need help, we are asked to initiate the first step (e.g., seeking out a doctor, then trusting that the right treatment and timing of procedures can occur).

Miracles by their very nature ask us to let GOD in, which means edging out our lower shadow energy, ego, and will. Today, be open to what seems impossible, but also notice the small miracles happening in every moment of the day. Indeed, you yourself are a miracle; you matter and illuminate this world. To God, who loves you, every step you take is a wonder, and every feat you accomplish is celebrated. Welcome to the miracle of life itself today.

NEW VINTAGE

BE OPEN MINDED

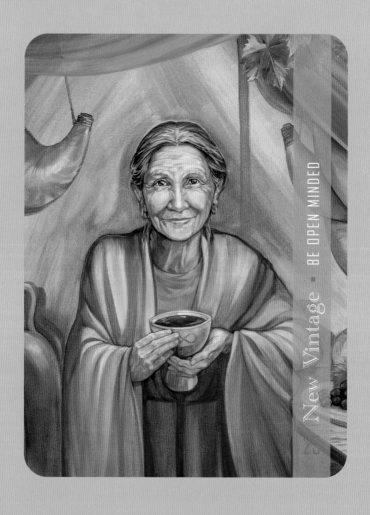

To truly drink from the cup of life is to understand that to stay open to new ideas, new perspectives, and other ways of being keeps you young in body, mind, and soul. Right now, it is important to stay inquisitive, curious, and eager to learn, and to greet each new day afresh, with no expectations of how it will be, but rather what it could be. Jesus used the parable of new wine needing to be put into new skins (bottles), since older skins would fail to hold the liquid. This liquid though is our ever-evolving consciousness and spirit; we are warned not to become stuck, intransigent, or rigid in what we think possible, or how we expect the world to be. Being inflexible to new ideas is a characteristic that can affect young and old alike. Here we see in this card the Wine Seller, who, although an elder, is alive with youth and vigor, her eyes full of wisdom, experience, and desire to find out more. You are reminded to never lose your love for life, your ability to serve, and your desire to see beyond what you already know.

A supple mind and open heart are the main requirements and a willingness to engage in life, not hide away, stagnate, or simply stay too close to your comfort zone. So often we stay with what is safe and predictable rather than giving ourselves the opportunity to meet new people, engage in different activities, and broaden our interests. This may be linked to any area of life, career, and relationships, but also our mindset and beliefs. Your soul came here to enjoy the rich variety of experiences that can be found only on Earth; to limit yourself to just one tree from which to pick fruit in God's Garden deprives you of so much.

This card also suggests that there are elders in your family or circle with the answers that you seek. From their life experience, particular journey, and skill set, they have guidance to offer you at this time. They may be a parent, grandparent, neighbor, friend, or teacher. They're likely still alive, but also you can draw on ancestors, guides, and sacred knowledge passed down from generation to generation, since everything is new to ears that have never heard it before.

You also are held by the ancient ones as you peel back layers of previous understanding to find deeper truths, new teachings, and fresh ways of understanding your life. Leave no stone unturned as you enjoy browsing libraries of new information, and be interested in the questions that are provoked and the areas that are challenged. You are ready for the next level of teaching, and much of this comes from walking the path. Christ Consciousness living will take you to places and people that will test you to see whether you can stay in your heart.

See your life as a canvas on which there are already brushstrokes, but onto which new colors and patterns wish to arrive. Some will be mysterious and complex and some simple and straightforward, but all make up the greater picture of your life.

Right now, be light-footed; flow, and see where life takes you and what awaits around the next corner. Endeavor to enjoy being life's eternal student, drinking from its cup and freely knowing more will come. To look back at a life well lived is the road to travel, so today explore all you can, for tomorrow another surprise will await.

PURITY

RETURN TO INNOCENCE

Purity · RETURN TO INNOCENCE

26

To remain of pure heart and mind at this time is emphasized, as well as being open to being showered in springtime colors and a burst of yellow vibrational joy. We live in a world with distractions and energies that often lower and dent our view of reality. Clouds come and blot our inner landscape, and we can become jaded, cynical, and despondent. We can start to anticipate and therefore attract the next thing to go wrong, feeling that life is somehow conspiring against us. Such distortion may come from disappointments, from betrayal, or via being worn out by life and its demands, expectations, and pace.

You may have once felt enthusiastic and ready to greet each day afresh but now are seeing life through dulled eyes. Pulling this card asks you to look again and see the world afresh, just as children are born curious and inquisitive, seeing goodness in everything; you too are reminded of this more innocent pure state. It exists within others and inside you; that spark of pure light that you incarnated with and that no event, person. or situation has ever truly vanquished.

Spending time with young children and animals can assist you now by helping lift your spirits and overall well-being. Being close to the energy of both is important: hearing children play, their voices in happy song; watching newborn lambs and the fish in the pond. Nature helps rekindle what we seek from the first raindrops of spring and the return of migrating birds, all heralding a new cycle where we can start again. Moments that remind us of the cycle of life, the energy of birth, and the promise it always brings. The tentative exploration and wonder of a child's first steps, the first feed, the harmony of making flower garlands, and the imprints of a winter's first snow angel.

Additionally, the prospect of rebirth is seen in those close to death, for the soul is always reborn anew, casting off the shackles and ailments of a body that has run its natural course. We enter life as pure spirit, and we are welcomed back after death as such. While here, we must not forget we are spirit within a body that came to run freely in God's Garden, and note that it was good.

It may also be time to look at healing a heart that has hardened and become suspicious, doubting people's motives and intentions and blocking positive opportunities from arriving. To keep the heart energy soft and open is to keep it pure, since the greatest protection is to emit such a strong frequency of light that no darkness can touch it, just as Jesus taught. Today, take a walk or sit by a window and just marvel at creation, take breaths of clean air into your lungs, and notice the water and skies, the birds in the air, the rustle of a tree, the clouds, and the scent of life. All these things and more put us closer to the one that created it and thus nearer to Purity and the healing available.

Meditate and reflect on the energies of Purity and Innocence, ask to receive downloads of both, and feel as their respective rays touch your heart deeply and transform your view of the world, and the goodness within it.

27

UNITY

COEXISTENCE & TOLERANCE

Unity · COEXISTENCE & TOLERANCE

27

We all say we seek a unified peaceful world, and yet, the truth is that to achieve that goal we must start with ourselves, to hold peace and unity within, and in our everyday life. If we are not able to do this, we will be scattered, since every part of everything is reflected within us. So today, feel into where are you feeling an absence of unity. It may manifest via trying to put on a brave face, or it could be an unexpressed emotion, interest, or desire, something you truly wish to be or do but are unable to freely express or show yet.

Very often we can present the face others wish to see, not always how we truly are deep down. What once may have worked may no longer fit, and within relationships, "putting on a united front" for others can hide pain also.

Within a family group, there may be arguments, misunderstandings, or disagreements over how to handle or deal with an issue. There may also be aggravation caused by neighbors, business colleagues, new family members, or a new person who alters the status quo. Anything that encroaches on our energy and disturbs our inner balance is relevant, since when we are in harmony, we feel at peace and can maintain an inner order. A misconception is that unity means we must agree on everything, whereas living in unity is about being tolerant, being able to coexist, and being open to listen, and for the same courtesy to be extended back to you. Whatever needs healing now, see it as an opportunity to bring parts of yourself together or others together. It may not be an easy or straightforward path, but working from the heart and for the right reasons for all concerned will be a rewarding one.

For yourself, it may be about balancing Mind, Body, and Soul. You might have been concentrating on spiritual matters at the expense of your physical body and neglected some aspect of self-care. Or it could be that the physical world is too dominant, obsessions with body image, fitness, and aging at the expense of inner spiritual work.

With those around you, you may be asked to be peacekeeper or peacemaker and be the bridge (e.g., the one to start discussions, organize an outing or meet up, extend the olive branch, and draw a line in the sand to create a fresh start).

There is work for all of us to do on quelling the inner wars we have within, which left unhealed contribute to outer wars in our world too. We may be at war with our parents, an ex-partner, or a cause or political position that we rail against. We may also hold prejudices and unhealthful past dogma that distorts how we look at the world and others. Starting to truly see each person you meet as a soul brother or sister radically changes our interactions.

Last, we need to make peace with Mother Earth to appreciate all that she gives, to live in harmony with her, plant trees, clear her rivers, look after our patch of land, and share what we have. Working toward seeing everything as part of a greater whole with the interconnectivity of all life, leaving this world a better place for the next generation to come.

FAITH

FIND HOLINESS WITHIN

Faith · FIND HOLINESS WITHIN

28

This card is inspired by the story of a woman who had been suffering from hemorrhages for 12 years. Seeing Christ in a crowd, she reached out and touched His gown and immediately knew that the source of her illness had ceased, since she knew "that even if I touch His clothes, I shall be cured." At first glance, this story makes us think that it was Jesus himself who healed her, but turning to the crowd and asking who had touched Him, He said to her, "It was your faith alone that cured you." It is an important distinction and one that is needed to be heard by many who believe that someone, something, or only a higher power can heal them. In this teaching it is clear the power lies within you and your ability to have faith, and that this alone is enough.

So often we look outward for help, guidance, and the answers, yet you are reminded that you have the power and tools you need.

The question needing to be asked is "Can I touch holiness within myself?" To do so is to be able to access all that you seek and your ability to find balance, and to know that all is well. Illness and challenge can also teach and instruct us and others; the soul grows through what it experiences on Earth; it is why it came. In the highlighted story the afflicted woman had sought many remedies and counsel from others, and yet these years were not without worth, since we often find out how strong we are via surviving adversity, pain, and difficulty. That is not to say it is what God wants for us, but to be human is to have agreed to walk this path, which can have thorns as well as the scent of the rose. "Into every life a little rain must fall" is a well-known saying, but it is also a true one.

Healing can also occur via encouragement and support to keep going. We are often carried even when we do not recognize it, feeling as though our prayers have been ignored, but it is often then when God is in fact closest.

We all seek the miracle and healing cure, and this can be possible if it is what the body, mind, and soul truly desire, but all aspects have to be in agreement for this to happen. So often we listen only to what one part of us wants, but if we instead see ourselves as multidimensional beings, we tune into different needs and requirements for soul growth.

Today, take a deep breath and think about how you can access holiness within. Certainly, giving yourself quiet space and room to just "be" is helpful: prayer, writing, or any activity that quiets the egoic mind is good. Finding holiness in everyday events encourages us to see each interaction as an opportunity to touch God, because everything is part of His creation and holds the frequency of love. Love is the greatest healer, and we must not lose faith with it or become so blindsided by negativity or displeasure that we fail to see it available in every moment. To turn a grimace into a smile, a clenched fist into an embrace, and a battle cry into a lullaby. When we can answer life with love, we see it returned to us tenfold. The lady reaching for Christ's gown knew He was complete love; it was that vibration and the trust in it that saved her. Reach for the love within yourself too, shower yourself with its healing balm, and visit the inner sanctuary and library of your heart that knows all the answers you seek. Love and Faith move mountains, so move some today.

HOLY GRAIL

SACRED UNION

To come into union with oneself is the greatest love and creates new worlds that can manifest outwardly, including loving relationships that are pure, holy, and sacred. It always starts first as an inner journey and pilgrimage, and within the template of Jesus and Mary Magdalene we have two energies to bring into our hearts, integrate, and learn from.

Mary, not the outcast, sinner, or fallen woman but the one Christ loved most, the one whom He first revealed Himself to at the tomb, and the disciple who understood Him the most. Within her He found a kindred soul, a confidant, and a beloved equal; not a relationship of imbalance but one of alliance, shared understanding, commitment, and unswerving loyalty. In Jesus, Mary found a friend, an anointed love, a shared purpose, passion, kinship, and wisdom. Her yin to His yang, His yang to her yin, together creating a portal, safe dwelling ground, and forward-flowing movement for generations to come.

This card encourages you to explore the energies both of Mary and Jesus, the times they are recorded as having interacted and the times not written. For there is much more to be revealed, and the truth of it lies within reach, deep knowing of the power of Divine Masculine and Divine Feminine combined and how it transformed the world then and still can now.

The Vesica Pisces symbol between them illustrates the potential that exists when two fully formed whole energies intersect and create something new, unique, and unexplored. Such magic materializes out of space, time, and other dimensions; it is the birth that transcends and liberates all it touches.

You may be working on the creation of something new, be it a baby, a project, a skill, or craft, and to do so successfully requires the merging of both your feminine and masculine selves. This means to Do as well as to Care, to Focus as well as to Rest, to Proceed and make time to Pause, to be Clear and Direct but also Soft and Open. It is in this balanced energy that fertile new growth occurs that is sustainable, lasting, and true.

You may also be seeking healing within relationships, looking to understand the art of giving and receiving, being held, allowing space, opening, and allowing someone in. Additionally, you may feel as though sacred love is elusive and hard to find, having built up walls of mistrust or miscommunication for protection and to prevent yourself from getting hurt.

Again, you are encouraged to practice self-love, to heal the broken and damaged parts, and to learn to love yourself no matter what. Your worth is not based on anyone else's approval or recognition, since God loves you unconditionally, and if you do not love yourself, how can you expect another to? Jesus and Mary teach us how to truly acknowledge our divinity and presence, and they also urge you not to turn away from your scars or parts of yourself that you judge. None of us are perfect; our flaws, mistakes, and broken bits make us human.

The Holy Grail is found when we feel worthy of drinking from it, where we stand in our God-given sovereignty, beauty, and light. Then, we will have ceased looking for others to save or love us, and will realize that we have everything we need inside. This new understanding and incidence will then be mirrored back to us, a Divine Union, all that is holy unleashed to create the new.

GRATITUDE
APPRECIATION & THANKS

One of the fastest ways to raise our emotional state and vibration is through the daily practice of gratitude, since we all have something to be thankful for, including the life we were blessed to have been given.

Spending time today thinking about the people and things that bring you the most joy will help your heart to open and your energy to lift. It may be a family member, an anniversary or celebration you enjoy, the warmth of an unexpected loving embrace, your favorite place to visit, or an inspiring piece of music. Often when we are sad, bored, depressed, or going through hard times, it is easy to focus on what is amiss and may have gone wrong. Even if this is true, though, by dwelling on it needlessly, we lower our vibration, making it hard to manifest what we seek. We start to see life through a cloudy lens, expecting more problems rather than seeing the beautiful world it still can be.

Waking every morning being glad to see the sunrise or the morning rain shows our appreciation for Mother Earth and all she provides. Additionally, thanking God for the warm drink, food on our plate, doctors, emergency services, the roof over our head, and our necessities met is important, since we should never take anything for granted. What we have may be what another person so desperately needs.

If you are struggling with ill health, give thanks for what you can do, the parts that still work; indeed, often when one sense gets dulled, another can become more enhanced. You may not be able to hear, but you see or sense very deeply; you may not be able to walk, but your arms are strong, and you can sing like an angel. Honoring the physical body, which is the vessel in which your soul lives, is vital, as is showing it love rather than judgment. Even at the end of our lives, we should be grateful to our body, which took us through our earthly journey, and bless every part of it.

Practicing gratitude puts us in the present moment, since often we are racing ahead with what needs to be done, forgetting to stop and acknowledge our life happening now in this moment.

Families grow up fast, so savor the early years, the cuddles and tears, the first smile, the first day at school; they all are part of the blessing of being a parent, as well as the empty nest when you regain space and independence and can seek out new adventures. Even at times of loss, when we mourn we are asked to be grateful for what we once had, to see it as the gift that it was, and its memory still forever within your heart, precious times that never fade.

Think today about what really matters to you, what you live for, and what uplifts you; it may be the arrival of summer, the scent of fresh baking, the pet loyally at your feet, the fresh flowers in the vase, the handwritten letter from a loved one.

Giving thanks is also a way to strengthen your faith, because when you look at what you have been given, it helps us appreciate the universe as a loving abundant energy that wishes us well. We are taught "to give him (God) love and praise," and a main quality of this when living from Christ Consciousness is to remain grateful for the unconditional love that is bestowed on us, which always forgives, provides, and never gives up on us. For that alone we are truly blessed.

31

STAND UP
STEADFAST VISION

Jesus through His ministry had frequent occasions when He directly challenged the status quo and rulings of the day. He did so when He felt they were unjust and outdated, knowing that new times required new ways. He was not apathetic or timid; He spoke out in radical ways, triggering (although not His intention) those who refused to listen or entertain his teaching.

Right now, you may be feeing compelled to stand up for an injustice or cause that you hold dear. You may struggle to see the oppression, inequality, and poverty in our world and think, "What can I do?" Yet, we are all more powerful than we imagine, and when we lend our voice, presence, and support to something worthwhile, we help many. Often, we wait for someone else to make the first move, but even if no one else joins you, it builds your sense of who and what YOU are, impacting your legacy left for future generations. Think about what troubles you; it may be environmental, political, social, or something that you have experienced firsthand. You may have been shunned, misunderstood, vilified, or judged for something you hold true. It takes bravery to speak up and be seen, but like Jesus it can create waves that can lead to extraordinary change, if we are brave enough to stand up.

You will find there are others who share your vision of a better world, and the kinship and support of being with like-minded people at this time is helpful. A gathering of your soul tribe can happen online or in person and will make you feel a sense of belonging.

You may have felt quite alone and isolated, feeling as though few see the world as you do, and in truth to be sensitive and empathic is to care deeply compared to those who turn a blind eye.

You are here to help make a difference, to be an advocate for light, and to not be afraid, knowing you are protected and held as you endeavor to make a positive difference.

This card is also a nod to unity and coming together around a centralized point, be that peace, remembrance, freedom, or something else. Solidarity, steadfastness, and being together as one holds the promise Jesus taught of "where two or more are gathered in my name," miracles can happen.

This may also be a time when your unhealed aspects are being illuminated. This may have been stirred up by current stories in the collective media (e.g., victims of abuse, women's rights, sexual identity, racial inequality). A highlighted story can touch us and help identify a story, experience, or pain that needs to be heard and healed.

"The light shines in the darkness, and the darkness has not overcome it," in the first chapter of John's gospel, identifies the light that you have within you that can heal anything brought out of the shadows, as well as bringing understanding and peace.

Being around positive, motivated, uplifting people will also be beneficial at this time, not those seeking to derail or thwart your path and light via words, thoughts, or deeds. It may be advisable to review the company that you keep, but if needing to be around those, for example, with draining energy (via duty/responsibility), ensure you are spiritually shielded. You may be able to inspire them, but remember that we can't force or change anyone against their will. Just demonstrate loving action and change, which others can follow or not via their free will.

32

THE OPEN DOOR
CHRIST WITHIN YOU

Open Doorway awaits with accessibility to Christ's energy and guidance that is nondenominational, does not have to be tied to church or any institution, is compatible with any other belief system, and is your personal invitation to a closer connection to Him.

The door is never closed; it is not manned by anyone, and no one is barred entry. It is open to all, regardless of creed, color, class, and individual perspective. It also places no judgment on what you have been or done, and it holds no record of wrongdoing; rather, it celebrates your wish to elevate your consciousness and seek deeper spiritual nourishment. You are warmly welcomed; all that is required is that you dust off your feet and enter through its portal to Holy Ground. You may come alone or be carried by another, or you may bring someone, because there is room for all, and there will never be "no room available at the inn."

Here in its sacred pastures, you will find anything that you seek to bring you back to harmony and balance; this may be the reset you require, silence and stillness, or laughter and company. Whatever you need is here and always for your highest good.
You will want to become a better version of who you are now, inspired to be the best you can be, taking seriously your commitment to spiritual development and relishing the opportunity to evolve and grow in the presence of Christ.

During his time on Earth, Jesus never turned anyone away; He made Himself available to any person in need. When asked to heal a leper, He did; when with those judged by others, He gives them His undivided attention. He attended those in deep grief and when invited to happy occasions, He also gladly participated.

There is no part of your life that needs to be hidden from Him, and no aspect of who you are that bars you from Christ's love, attention, and care, nor any problem whether small or large. Do not allow fear or insecurity to alter what you think is possible, and do not let societal or family patterning think you cannot seek a personal connection with Jesus. Old-paradigm thinking taught you had to be chosen in some way or sacrifice something to gain His presence. But this is redundant and ego led; rather, He walks beside all who seek His company, time, and love, always appearing humbly to help serve you, seeing all as worthy and seeing their divinity within.

Right now, you are at this doorway in your life and are invited to open to something greater: to your connection to Him—either to deepen an existing connection or discover Him for the first time—and to your own Christ self. Allow the grace of love to sweep over you; soak into your skin, muscle, and bone, filling you with Christ light, strengthening and fortifying you for what is ahead and to come.

As your heart opens wider, it leads to further doorways and ever-expanding connection and experience until you realize that the church is you and your body is the temple, and that Christ Consciousness dwells there and has made a happy home. Here lives love, and it flourishes as you water it daily via prayer, reflection, good deeds, being there for others and tending to your own needs with care.

33

THE TEACHER
WALK THE TALK

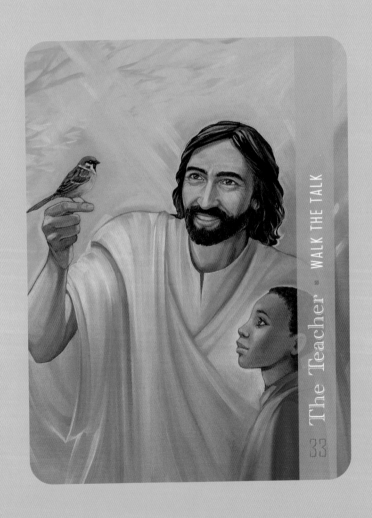

Much of Jesus's teaching came via what He did just as much as what He said. He walked the talk, demonstrating in every possible interaction the core thesis of what it looked like to hold Christ Consciousness. The large organizations and their buildings (albeit often beautiful) that followed can make us forget that in essence He taught us how to BE, and how to truly live a good and honest life. He was a teacher who wanted to be with people, working tirelessly and never faltering from the love that He demonstrated in everything His presence touched. He rightfully sits as one of this world's greatest masters, yet He reminds us that we can emulate and practice much of what He taught, and that it is achievable and not undoable.

He knows there are inevitable moments when you may have acted in ways you are ashamed of or said things that can't be undone. However, He does not see you as a "miserable sinner" needing to reimburse for these shortcomings, but instead encourages you to learn from mistakes, move on, and try again. When we start to understand why we reacted a certain way, we can begin the process to heal our wounds and triggers.

When we need help, Jesus will step forward to guide us, and He will never reprimand you. Rather, He sees you as a child of God who is still learning, and no one reprimands a child when they fall; they help pick them up and set them back on the right course. Realize also that having walked this earth Himself, He understands what it is to be human, the unique challenges that exist here from temptation to cruelty, injustice, inequality, and more. When He witnessed suffering, He went to help; when He knew trouble was unavoidable, He walked into the "arena" just as His followers did centuries later. He knew that God would never abandon Him, and likewise He will never abandon you; we are all truly blessed to have His assistance!

Jesus, now as spirit among us, guides you still, highlighting a path where your own Christ Consciousness can shine, and you too become a teacher for others. We all are life's teachers; the example we set is copied by, for example, our children, for good and bad, in terms of habits, patterns, and more. As Jesus said, it is by your acts you are known, and by loving one another you will be recognized as one of His disciples (meaning a student or follower). As such, we need to monitor our behavior in all areas of life; what we say anonymously (or not) online to someone we may not know is just as important as a face-to-face conversation with one we do. We should be consistent, knowing there is no area of life to which the principles of Christ do not apply . . . and in the hardest subjects (e.g., politics, finance, sexuality), we still need to be able to walk the talk and demonstrate our heart-centered consciousness in action.

Teaching comes from many places, via children and different cultures and places, and from hard times such as illness, in so many ways. We will constantly learn if we ask of anything, "What does this show me? What have I to learn from this situation?"

We are encouraged to become like children again, full of wonder, wanting to learn and acquire new understanding. The small child who asks, "Why" is inquisitive and keen to know!

Embrace being life's student as well as its teacher; we learn from each other, and via that our consciousness continues to grow.

34

HUMBLENESS
MODESTY & HUMILITY

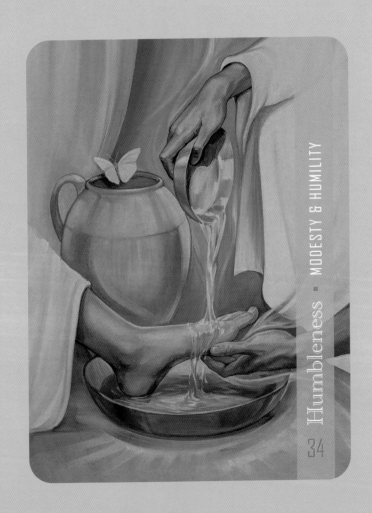

Humbleness · MODESTY & HUMILITY

34

Many of us live in cultures that from childhood constantly push us to aspire higher and achieve more. Material possessions and positions of power are held in esteem; the CEO of a company is held in better regard than other "lesser" roles. But this is old-paradigm thinking; we all need each other to keep the wheels of our world turning. Humbleness and humility as qualities can be overlooked at the expense of ego-led drivers that will, it is assumed, achieve more faster. This, however, needs reexamining, since to champion instead quiet virtue, diligence and grounded authenticity are key.

Become aware of the moments we get to serve this world in small ways and larger ones. From the tending of the overgrown garden helping nature to flourish, to the baking of bread to feed our families. If we can consciously address each task and moment as an opportunity to demonstrate Christ Consciousness, we contribute so much more than we realize, particularly when we do it with love. To not judge anything as more worthy of our time or attention; the cleaning of a home or the washing of clothes is just as important as the pressing work assignment or challenging project.

In the washing of the disciples' feet by Jesus, He demonstrated that no job is too lowly or unworthy and that no one is more important than another. Indeed, in acts such as these, we truly show our greatness, not via sitting in lofty positions of esteemed value. In the times of Jesus, washing of the feet before a meal would have been conducted by more-lowly servants; Jesus, however, demonstrated clearly that He was happy to do this and did so as an act of love as well as to help. He also carried it out to set an example for others to follow. The cleansing aspect of washing the feet is also a prompt to keep ourselves clean physically, mentally, emotionally, and spiritually. We should take notice of where our feet take us, into what territory and with which intent; to walk in peace is the goal.

Recognizing what we do not know is also an aspect of humbleness, since there will always be more to learn and new discoveries to be revealed. Keeping any sense of superiority in check is vital, since we all are students of life and the journey eternal. To not be arrogant or proud but to go about our life quietly and diligently knowing we are loved and noticed for who we are is also an important aspect of humbleness.

Today, reappraise neglected areas of your life that you deemed unimportant or had not prioritized: the phone call you had put off, as well as community activities (e.g., the beach/park cleanup to volunteer for, or charity items to donate). This card can also be an invitation to offer back random acts of kindness with no expectation for acclaim or recognition, a goodwill gesture that will brighten another's day.

Appreciate also how caring for those under your care is a privilege, not a chore; both the baby and the elderly parent with needs that can be answered with a humble heart, remembering that you too have once been that baby and you too will be the old man or woman.

To give with no pretense or agenda, simply from love, is one of the highest acts of spiritual service we can give. Kindhearted acts and helping those who are struggling show our humility and what is best in being human.

35

ENLIGHTENMENT

CONTINUE TO GROW

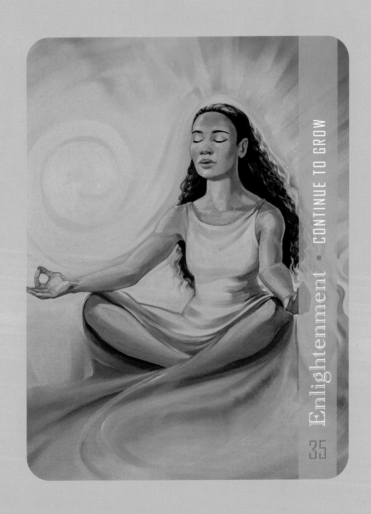

"In my father's house there are many rooms" is a teaching from Jesus, and one we should remember when we consider the nature of enlightenment. In God's house (i.e., the Kingdom of Heaven, which also exists on Earth), all are welcome, diversity is encouraged, and different faiths and beliefs are equally respected, reflecting that all the Ascended Masters work together, and that man-made divisions are redundant. Here there should be no condemnation or suspicion of how others experience Spirit and God, or any desire to be right and the only one holding the truth. Instead, we are invited to sit energetically in circle with our fellow brothers and sisters to witness each other's journeys underneath the same "roof," which is our world that we are here to experience. We can learn from each other and grow as we seek to deeply understand, listen, and engage.

In essence, there is not just one way to experience God. Christ Consciousness's qualities are shared by many who seek to put love, forgiveness, and compassion center stage, and we need to remember that we all come from and go back to the same energy of creation, which is love. Realize too that at any one time we will all be working on different parts of the enlightenment path, requiring tolerance of each other, since what you may have mastered, others will be just learning and vice versa. We also are seldom aware of others' soul contracts and lessons already completed in their other lives. Wherever we are now, though, will require introspection of ourselves, absolute honesty, and a willingness to adapt, change, and be open to what arises. So often there is a misconception that spirituality is just about love and light, and while these ARE the most-powerful energies at our disposal, we become truly enlightened only by being brave enough to go into our own darkness and shadow. Here there is no escape from our flaws, selfish acts, and unkindness; we must face unpleasant truths about ourselves, what we have done, thought, and been. God never judges these parts, however, and neither should we stay in shame, but instead bring love into our pain and ugliness to heal, enlighten, and transform the hidden corners of self and all we are.

Acknowledge the sacred inner journey you are on, one that can be helped via self-care practices, reflection, mindfulness, meditation, fresh fruit and vegetables, and perhaps yoga or another form of holistic exercise. By going within, we understand more of what manifests outward as a result, seeing the mirror effect of what we are and can then attract into our lives. We become more conscious, in tune with our surroundings and environment, and realize the influence we can assert positively to raise the vibration of Earth as well as ourselves.

Today, think about whether you are spiritually growing or in a safe zone or are stuck, unable to expand into new ideas and ways to interact with the world. Is there something you wish to learn, an imbalance that needs correction (e.g., in receiving or giving, or a new practice you would like to try)? Be willing to sit and absorb the frequency of Mother Earth as she ascends in consciousness too, receiving her light codes, moon phases, cyclical dates, and changing rhythms.

Being at one with your body's energy system and listening to its needs helps you respect the temple that holds your soul in this lifetime and serves you well.

TETHERED & CAGED
BREAK FREE

Choosing this card today suggests that you or someone around you may be struggling to escape from a manipulative, toxic, or lower energy that keeps them captive in destructive relationships or dysfunctional thinking, behaviors, and situations. It may be linked to addiction, repetitive cycles, and being attracted to what is unhelpful or unwise. Alternatively, sometimes we choose to avert our gaze from what needs attention due to fear of what it will entail and whether we have the strength required to break free. However, the overwhelming compulsion that something we are tied to is stronger than Christ's light that we hold inside us is totally untrue. These darker energies may be compelling, attractive, and tempting. What once started off as experimentation, fun, and curiosity can trap us into set mindsets and actions.

The addict is one who believes only the next fix matters, be it drugs, alcohol, food, sex, work, or gambling (and there are many addictions). Most of us have unhealthful attachments to something, including lower energies such as gossip, projection, and denial. In truth, anything that separates us away from our god-given right to live a good, happy, and free life is devil energy. Not the devil with two horns, but the darkness that we can unintentionally invite in to entertain us to fill up the hole and vacuum where our own power, strength, and divinity should lie. There is often an open unhealed wound that leaves us vulnerable to, for example, people with false promises, quick-fix answers, something "too good to be true," or just the desire to smother and cover up the wound with anything "to make it go away."

It is also linked to the inability to see the beauty and joy in life, having our head filled with doom and worst-case scenarios, and focusing on what could go wrong and our inability to avoid it. We may be reading and watching material that has lowered our vibration, unable to discern the intention with which it is created and shared. It may take us into a plane of unrelenting misery and an alternate reality. This can also be via endless submersion into, for example, violent video games and simulated dark artificial worlds.

Again, balance is key, and we need to ask ourselves, "Is this helpful? Is it constructive?" "Can I learn something from it, and does it show me lessons and the way back to the light?" If the answers to all the above are no, it is wise to change course and, like the sunflower, turn your head toward what is light again to nourish you.

The truth is we are never really trapped if we tap into the power we have within; there is always a way out, and spiritual help is available. The key is there to unlock our shackles if we just look up and reach for the light.

Today, strive to remove yourself from the source of your discomfort; this may necessitate big or small changes to your everyday life, but it starts with acknowledging what is out of balance and taking small steps toward a new way of being. A new chapter beckons that is more healthful, happier, and more in tune with who you really are. Ask Christ to show you the way and to take your hand as you follow His template to lead the life you truly deserve and of which you can be proud. Be gentle with yourself today; you are loved and are stronger than you think.

37

JOSEPH OF ARIMATHEA

TRAILBLAZE & INNOVATE

Joseph of Arimathea • TRAILBLAZE & INNOVATE

37

To understand this card's message, we need to appreciate who Joseph of Arimathea was and why his energy around you now is important. Joseph was a rich Jewish man, a member of the ruling Sanhedrin (council) as well as a secret disciple of Jesus. Some believe he was also a great uncle of Jesus. As a benefit of high rank and his contacts, Joseph asked Pilate if he could take Jesus down from the cross, and upon permission he wrapped His body in linen shrouds and laid Him in the garden tomb. This much is agreed by all four Gospel writers. In other ancient texts he is said to have been imprisoned for his actions but freed after receiving a visitation from Jesus too. Centuries later, legends linking Joseph to the Holy Grail (Last Supper cup), planting his pilgrims' staff into Wearyall Hill, where it rooted as the Holy Thorn tree (still in existence today), and creating the first church in England in Glastonbury. There are also stories of Joseph bringing Jesus to England himself as a younger man. In fact, the English hymn "Jerusalem" is a nod to "ancient feet walking England's Green and Pleasant land."

Currently, Joseph's life and energy are calling YOU to fresh pastures, to tread new ground, possibly to travel physically or in your mind, to plant fertile seeds, or to be the "first" to do or say something. Doing so may necessitate breaking out of old templates, family conditioning, and beliefs of what you think you can achieve. You are encouraged to be brave in forging new relationships, alliances, and experiences, starting either from zero point or with some aspects already known. It may be that the path you carve inspires others to follow your example, influencing ideas and stimulating new energy. Recognize too that you will be helped to build solid foundations and a practical framework to succeed. You would not be encouraged by spirit to change, adapt, or begin again if you would meet failure.

There is also a nod to legacy with this card and what you will leave behind after you die. The spirit who you were, of course, lives on; what you stood for, championed, and built can all remain, including the impact you had on other people's hearts and minds. To be remembered fondly with gratitude is what we all aspire to, and as such we need to live being conscious of our behavior and energy.

We all make our mark upon this earth; we all plant "staffs" to a degree, whether it be through our children, our family, creative endeavors, projects, or memories that are everlasting.

We may not all be tasked with the job that Joseph was given, to create the first church, but we do all take on important soul missions in some form, and our energy, life, and presence spreads God's light in ways we often fail to notice.

We may also want to carry on traditions, talents, and gifts in our ancestral line; to cultivate musical gifts, healing arts, and interests that others have loved or excelled at. We may unconsciously continue where our ancestors left off: the boy who picks up his father's trade or interest, or the daughter who succeeds at college, where her own father was never given the opportunity.

Each generation builds on the previous, creating something bigger and better that enriches the world and themselves. Allow Joseph to help you with life's transitions as the shepherd who knows where you need to be, what needs attending to, and offers practical help guiding you and making sure no stone is left unturned. Your new life awaits; plant the seeds now for your future that is already assured.

38

FREEDOM

JUST BE YOU

Freedom • JUST BE YOU

38

Jesus's energy is one of freedom—as a man over 2,000 years ago, He broke away from many of the expected traditions and norms of His day. To some He was a revolutionary, to others a threat, but for many He quenched their appetite to move beyond old structures, thoughts, and goals. He saw beyond what already existed and was a trailblazer for new ways. Holding Christ Consciousness will see you too as someone who pushes against that which is unjust, as well as asking you to stand up for those who are forgotten and ignored. You will be asked to see the higher picture, be the better person, be able to let things go, and detach where necessary from that which doesn't serve you, often going against the crowd to do so.

All of this is helped by embodying a free sense of being, and it is important to remember that this is also a state of mind, not always an actual external expression. In other circumstances, we can be free even when imprisoned by circumstances beyond our control or shackled in some other form (e.g., by political oppression, financial restriction, or physical incapacity). True freedom is linked into holding the peace that Christ Consciousness teaches, having no malice, staying in alignment to our hearts, and knowing that our lives are eternal, and we are divinely loved.

In addition, freedom lies in grasping that you are truly a child of the universe; your soul cannot be contained by any one experience or incarnation, and there are multiple times and excursions to discover all that it is to be human. Indeed, God wishes you to have free reign to explore as much as you can, and has given us our senses through which to do that.

You may be in a situation, relationship, or job where you don't feel free, but the lesson is that this is illusion. You are where you are meant to be for what you are currently learning, but you always have the key to change anything and, like the bird in the cage, can fly out and be free. This flight of freedom occurs when you have moved beyond what no longer serves you, and acknowledged its reason for being present and the learning acquired.

Having a bird's-eye view of your life can clearly show you the parts that are worn out or needing attention. This can also include how we treat ourselves—are we imprisoned by destructive habits and behaviors, routines, and our own negative thoughts? If we can adopt a new course of action, then new outcomes can be found, and healing discovered. Your spirit wishes to break free, to register as much as possible every day, to make an impact on others and enjoy all there is to be savored, because life is meant to be joyous.

Freedom is also about discarding what others expect you to be, and embracing all you are, including the age and life stage you are at, your needs, and more. You may be living someone else's script of how your life should be, via a job, belief system, persona, or anything else. Release it now and any guilt, as when we have surrendered, we find ourselves in flow and will be taken to where we need to go. Just as the hot-air balloons ride the thermal to navigate the journey, be like the balloon that travels safely with a light load, not weighed down by excess baggage—it has the ability to soar as well as the ability to come in for a soft landing, replete from its experience and enjoyable excursions.

39

SPIRITUAL PROTECTION

ARMOR OF GOD

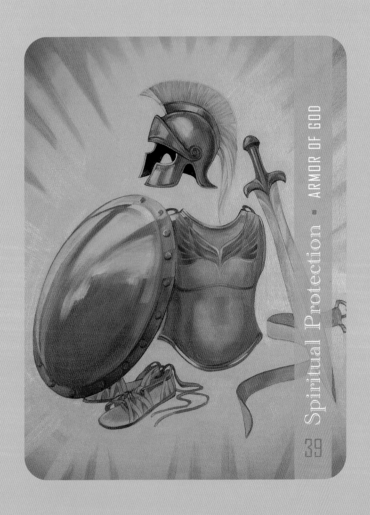

Spiritual Protection · ARMOR OF GOD

39

Walking in Christ Consciousness is to hold the most powerful light within you that steers, protects, and is a constant shield. It is not that you are invisible to darkness, but that it cannot penetrate or interfere with your energy field. This light you carry can never go out or be vanquished if we stay in our hearts and walk in the energy and follow the example of Christ. The template laid down is clear: at no point did Jesus either fear or succumb to any power that tried to subvert or derail Him, not when tempted or at His lowest ebb; He always stayed true to the light within. It is now your job to honor this light, nourish it, and allow it to shine at full velocity, fearing nothing and knowing all is well.

There is nothing that is stronger than the energy of this light, yet it is human to doubt and at times be overwhelmed by man's dark deeds and the evil and fear that are in our world. Yet, we are not defenseless or naked and vulnerable to those who seek to deceive, manipulate, or do us harm. We are given assurance that we will be looked after as a good Father looks after his children. This does not mean that no difficulty can befall us; it simply means God will always have our back. Sometimes bad things happen, but knowing that nothing can defeat you, that you are stronger than any attack or injustice, is vital to remember. If we look at the story of Jesus and His disciples, they suffered persecution, yet their inner courage and steadfastness is a key feature to all their journeys, where they maintained their light to the very end, since even death cannot destroy that.

As well as walking in light, you are also given the Armor of God, six pieces of energetic holy equipment with deep symbolism that can be put on daily to aid you and protect. The six pieces are

the Helmet of Salvation (Awakening)
the Breastplate of Righteousness
the Belt of Truth
the Shield of Faith
the Sword of the Spirit
Sandals for feet that walk in Peace

In the morning, ask for Jesus or your Higher Self to place these upon you, feeling the reassurance that comes via "putting on" each piece. With your armor on, you then can get on with your day, mindful of what you give attention and energy to, understanding that we can attract what is in our thoughts. It is therefore unhealthful to fret or invest too much time toward external dark energies, since you give them power by believing them so!

Staying around positive good people, energies, and situations is also a way of protecting ourselves. Think about all the things you surround yourself with and ask, "Are they healthful, life affirming, and helpful or are they draining, toxic, and negative?" Taking ownership of our environment, who is with us, and what we do makes us accountable to what we allow into our space. Staying pure in heart, seeing the divine in others, practicing the tenants of Christ Consciousness all raise our vibration, the most effective protection there is, and one that will never fail you.

40

LIVING FROM
THE HEART
SOFTEN & OPEN

Living from the Heart · SOFTEN & OPEN

40

To understand what living from the heart is, we need to appreciate first what it is not. The Gospels make clear that a hardened heart is one that cannot see or hear God; then not only do we fail to understand the consequences of our actions, but we are blind and deaf to being able to witness how God can work through any situation, event, or person. This is particularly true when faced with a challenge where we immediately block the opportunity for breakthrough and instead focus on the problems that are there. The disciples are admonished for being unable to see or understand even after they have seen miracles previously happen in the same circumstances. When faced with tainted yeast from Herod and the Pharisees, they worry about having no bread until Jesus reminds them of the Feeding of the 5,000!

Living from the heart therefore is about trust and being able to see the highest potential, the path through which God can work even in the most unseen or unlikely places. In our own lives it is too easy to self-sabotage, have doubts, be unclear, or focus on unwinnable odds. Yet, if we soften our hearts and open to see and hear God, we hold the key that makes anything possible.

The heart is also the mechanism through which we both give and receive. It stands to reason that if we have closed our hearts due to fear, past circumstance, skepticism, and more, we will fail to be able to receive the gift, bounty, and way out of our predicament.

Ego, pride, and foolishness too can prevent us from receiving the answers and help we seek. This can also arise from falling into victim consciousness, the belief that "nothing good ever happens to me" or that "I am unlucky or undeserving in some way." Jesus always taught that everyone was deserving of love, and our heart has not forgotten this promise.

The adage to trust our heart is one we have all heard but often fail to put it into practice. We doubt our heart can be correct when we feel or intrinsically know something or are prompted to try something new, visit somewhere, or try out for a new job or role. Living from the heart is about recognizing that God works through these promptings, signs, and feelings and that we are not wrong to trust them.

In truth, when our hearts are as fully open as the lotus flower, life is richer and we send healing and pollinate the world with love, resulting in Christ Consciousness in action. One open heart can open another, and so it continues, because when we are a witness for love we create a chain reaction that helps balance and harmonize our world.

To live from the heart necessitates us being vulnerable sometimes. We will also come up against those who are closed and intransigent, and may well be triggered by our goodness, since shining a light can make others very aware of their own lack of brilliance. Staying humble and nonjudgmental and holding compassion while the messy part of evolving takes place, for us and others, is key. The lotus grows and must push through mud to show its beauty, becoming one of the most stunning flowers. And as such, we too can burst out of our difficulties, limited mindsets, and ego and arrive at the heart's portal to birth new worlds today.

41

FAITH OVER FEAR
YOU CAN COPE

Faith over Fear ▪ YOU CAN COPE

The story of Jesus calming the storm is well known. It is said that as the storm unexpectedly arrived, the frightened disciples woke Jesus from His sleep for fear of being drowned, but after He calmed the wind and waves, He rebuked them for having little faith. At first glance this may seem insensitive; they were frightened, so why were they chastised? However, what was really being demonstrated was tough love to teach them that their fear was bigger than their faith, and it was that which was the bigger problem rather than the raging sea. Jesus was reminding them of the immense power, resourcefulness, and capability within themselves, which is amplified when we stay connected to God, who never leaves us. When we remember this fact, we have less reason to worry and fret because we understand we are divinely guided and always helped.

Think about "storms" that have arrived in your life and how you have handled them. Were you able to trust and have faith, or did you panic and allow fear to dictate how you responded? We must remember also that if we feed fear, it grows and can make anything worse. Sometimes we can spend days worrying over what may happen rather than working toward creating a better timeline.

It is human to be afraid, and at times we all are, but do we allow it to control and thwart us or do we rise above it and reorient back toward the bedrock of our lives, which should be faith, knowing we can cope?

Do we truly believe and trust that we will be led to where we are meant to be and that we will be shown what we need to see? Creating endless "what ifs" and focusing on what is amiss also can weaken our mental state over time. Instead we are asked to be the peaceful eye of the storm and not add to the drama or difficulty even if others around us are in panic. We will be given the strength to cope with anything that life throws at us, including, for example, divorce, illness, grief, trauma, or any hardship. God walks beside us throughout it all and is never truly "asleep." Also know that "this too will pass"; times may be rocky and upsetting, but better days will come.

Build up a memory bank also of the times you have faced your fears and survived, flourishing even when you thought you would not, when help came from nowhere after your prayers were heard. It is easy to have faith when life is easy, but when times get tough, this is when we can truly put it into practice rather than abandon what we stand for and believe in.

The miracle of calming the waters and wind also feels symbolic of us being able to balance our emotions (water) and thoughts (air), to be masters of our own "ship," realizing that when we harmonize our inner state, this will be reflected in what will manifest externally. We can create calm "waters" or "raging seas." Feeding our fear or feeding our faith is a choice we get to make; it takes practice to respond from a place of assuredness and strength, helped each time by the cumulative effects of choosing faith over fear.

Seek to build up your divine, knowing that all is well and that you are equipped for any eventuality, unexpected or planned, in your life.

42

GENTLENESS

RESPOND SOFTLY

Gentleness · RESPOND SOFTLY

The answer you seek right now is gentleness, to yourself and to the world. To bring in the energy of a mother's gentle embrace as the answer to pain, suffering, hardship, and the intolerable. You may feel overwhelmed, not knowing how to carry on or cope, yet the inner strength and fortitude sit within to weather any hardship and heal it with love. To be gentle in touch, sensitive to your needs and those of others, to use gentle words, a soft gaze, a gentle response rather than one driven by trying to fight it right.

You may have used up considerable energy trying to find a way, seek an answer, struggle on against innumerable odds, and battle the system, people, situations, and more, but now you need to rest, compose, gather your thoughts, and allow the universe to bathe you in healing and light.

The woman in the painting is clothed in violet, a color that brings balance and helps us attune to higher powers, including those within ourselves, creating a sanctuary of inner order and peace of mind. You may find it helpful to tune into the violet ray today, allowing it to comfort you, maybe via lavender flowers, scent, or visualizing it in meditation. It can soothe an overstimulated mind and reduce stress and tension too.

You may feel alone and unheard, cast out, ignored, or misunderstood, yet the calling to go within and settle any mental turmoil is recommended. You may not have all the answers you seek yet spend a moment soothing and calming yourself in what is often a chaotic world. It may also be that your own inner child is crying out to be heard and held, broken or wounded parts of yourself that now are coming up for healing. Know that this is the perfect opportunity to answer anything that demands your attention from your past, and respond to it with love, care, gentleness, and time. Surrendering and asking for help, knowing that it will arrive after being humbly requested, is also a current theme.

In addition, you may have a strong humanitarian heart, caring deeply about the world's suffering and pain, and there may be a particular story or ongoing situation that has deeply affected you. The plight of refugees, war, natural disasters, and many other aspects of our world have an impact on a caring, gentle heart such as yours. How to respond without becoming drained may be a hard balance to navigate, but knowing that every day in some small way we can make a difference is true. You are not here to take on all the world's problems, since this would be too much for anyone; just respond with love when you can, and be there for others, knowing that "there but for the grace of God go I."

Creating a world that Christ would be proud of, where we truly love each other, is an ongoing task but not one you undertake alone. You may be called to help at this time, offering support, wisdom, prayer, and resources to those who need it most, knowing these moments matter when we don't turn away. Do this, but also make sure you treat yourself with the same care you extend outward, the inner and the outer in harmony wanting to be heard and healed.

43

DISCERNMENT
TRUTH & CLARITY

Discernment · TRUTH & CLARITY

43

You may be faced with an issue where discernment is key, and you need to ascertain whether something is true, applicable, or aligned to your beliefs. It may be something you have read, heard, or seen, but be careful that someone else's opinions are not distorting your own intuition and wisdom. Our body's hunches and gut feelings are wonderful barometers as to whether something or someone is good for us or not. However, often we can be swayed by what others are doing rather than following our own instincts. You may also have a dilemma that leaves you confused or uncertain, not yet having all the information you seek, so ask for a sign or for what needs to be revealed to be shown to you.

Sometimes we must face what is uncomfortable; this can be about our own behavior, weaknesses, or wounding. We may not want to face our grief or destructive habits for fear it may consume us. We may be unable to make difficult decisions, even if doing so will ultimately free or help us in the long run. We may also be blinded to someone else's faults, cruelty, or insensitivity, as well as being afraid of saying what needs to be expressed or disengaging from what we know is wrong.

We can ignore moral and ethical aspects that require attention, focus, time, and action. We can turn a blind eye to collective problems, such as our material consumption and the planet's needs, because we feel we can make little difference. Yet, if everyone turns away, nothing will change. New Earth is born via new paradigms and us caring enough to weed and take care of our own backyard, figuratively and literally.

When we take off the blindfold to see what truly requires attention, we may at first be overwhelmed. But our eyes soon adjust to new frequencies and ways of being; we learn through new practices and ways of being, and we discover we are always supported. This card can also signify uncertainty in showing who you really are, for fear of being judged or ridiculed. Stand strong and be seen, and know you are held as you become more of who you were born to be. In doing so, you help others find their courage and strength.

We should remember that walking in Christ Consciousness is not about turning our gaze away from what is problematic. Jesus mixed with people whom others rejected, refusing to abide by unjust laws and norms that deemed them outcasts. His conversation with a woman at the well shows Him unconcerned that she was drawing water alone (having been shunned for having five marriages), nor was He concerned about interacting with a Samaritan, being Himself a Jew. He saw who she truly was, since He had no blindfold on. In this and many other incidences in the Gospels He showed the importance of bearing witness to a person's potential, goodness, light, and beauty. We do that best when we can look past transgressions, mistakes, and someone's humanness and see their soul via their eyes.

You may also have a dilemma that leaves you confused or uncertain, not yet having all the information you seek, so ask for a sign or for what needs to be revealed to be shown to you. Signs can be anything, such as seeing a random feather, as depicted here, or anything that you give significance to, such as number sequences (e.g., 444, 222), all of which imply a code or meaning that you may link to it.

44

MARY

MOTHERING & NURTURE

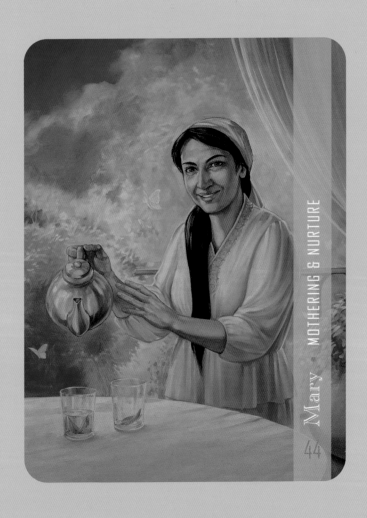

Mary · MOTHERING & NURTURE

44

Mother Mary has time for you when no one else does. She is your constant place to come back to for a warm embrace, a soft voice to coax you forward, a shoulder to cry on, and a place for lighthearted laughter and joy. Within her etheric space the table is always set, the tea waiting and the light on for whenever you need to visit and spend time with her. She does not judge, does not scold, has infinite patience, and has broad shoulders to help carry your burdens, as well as a heart bursting with pride for your triumphs and achievements. There is never anything too small or too big that you can bring to her door; she has heard it all before from the countless travelers from all corners of the globe that she serves. She never gets weary, never tires; her heart is enormous and open to all. Tapped into her divine light and grace, she not only is there to listen and be present but to model the qualities you seek in others as well as yourself.

To be patient and kind, forgiving and tolerant, constant, and steady, if Mary is the safe harbor to which you return, you are the "ship" made ready to go back out with sails mended, fuel in your tank, and a soft breeze to guide you on.

You may stay as long as needed in Mary's company, for convalescence through illness of body, mind, and soul or whatever troubles you. In her company you gain renewed strength and purpose, and the security of unconditional love.

You may call on Mary at any time: you may be struggling with issues linked to mothering, maybe how to be a good mother, becoming one, healing the relationship with your own, or having lost one. Some of you may never have known a mother's love, and Mary can teach and show you how to love and honor yourself. Never with judgment, always with understanding and knowing each soul tries to do the best it can in each incarnation. Healing the maternal line is also part of Mary's role, and she can help you unwind the tangled themes and challenges left there from times of old.

Mary operates at national and local levels, helping to heal issues for women everywhere, supporting the female creative power and strengthening nurturing qualities, which have the power to transform the world. She asks you to call her in to any group or gathering that needs a mother's touch.

You can never disappoint her, because she always is able to see the good in you, the times you have tried, the ways you have helped, even when it fell on deaf ears. She is not blind to your faults but sees them as unhealed parts and understands how hard it is to be human, the suffering and pain that can be part of our mission, just as it was for her raising Jesus as the little boy but seeing Him in agony on the cross. She encourages you to never waiver from seeing the higher plan and God's intentions, which are to experience life in its multifold ways and the roles we all play to walk each other home.

PAUL

AWAKENING &
TRANSFORMATION

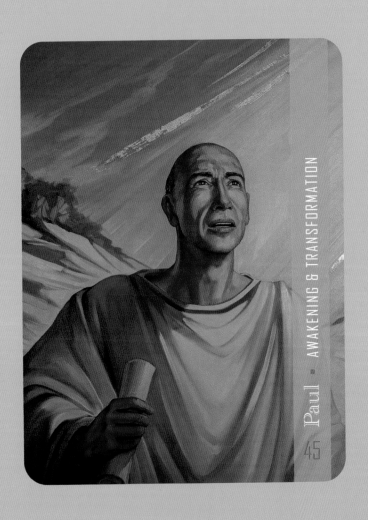

Just as Saul had a moment of revelation and moved away from a committed former way of life (changing his name to Paul), you also may be going through a similar time, with a new path beckoning. This new way may be the antithesis to how you have lived till now, and it may be totally new and an unchartered course, but like Paul it is about God having a bigger plan for you.

Awakening as Paul did with blinding light and hearing the voice of Jesus isn't something we all experience, but our transformation is just as real. It is important to remember that everyone's awakening is unique and takes many forms; signs can be subtle or extreme, and it can also come about via challenge and unexpected events. Sometimes it is our body that gives us signs; a breakdown or health battle can signal that the way we have been doing things is no longer sustainable. It may be a failed business, a job that no longer satisfies, a broken love affair, or simply a knowingness that something needs to change.

Like Paul, you may have stubbornly resisted something or have been unready to see how big changes could fit into or be part of your future. Be always grateful to your old self, though, for having gotten you this far with everything learned, since it will serve you well. For truly there is no such thing as a wrong path, since everything experienced teaches us something and adds to our ability to see situations from different perspectives.

As with Saul, this new you will transform others' perceptions as well; there may be skepticism, confusion, or suspicion that this new path is authentic and real. But stay true—so often we get held back because of what others want or expect us to be. Staying aligned instead to your new life demonstrates that change is possible for them too. It is important to trust that if you are being guided to change, help and the right people will arrive. In scripture we learn of Ananias, who is sent to heal Saul of his blindness, caused by his vision and blinding light on the road to Damascus. Ananias is fearful, knowing only the old Saul who persecuted mercilessly, but trusts God, who tells him he is a changed man. Both men are touched by the power of the moment and spirit moving through them, because awakening touches and transforms others, as it will for you in your life.

You may not yet know how the future will progress or what your next steps are, but trust that all will be provided and that the course is already set, and future success ensured.

As you say goodbye to old ways, behaviors, people, jobs, and identities, be aware that it can take time to settle into the new. This is to be expected and is made easier if you can firmly shut the door on the old. This may mean removing yourself from old, toxic associations, actions, or people. You take with you into the new only that which is supportive and true; there is no room for worn-out patterns or people that seek to thwart or pull you backward.

New friends, contacts, and experiences await that are beneficial, fruitful, and positive, and being clear about who you are now helps you commit to this new way of life, grounding, and anchoring it.

You may be surprised at how quickly things can change, how new insights and routines form. You are encouraged to look forward with renewed passion and zest for life. Awakening is always worth it.

46

LIONHEART

STAND FIRM

Being lionhearted means to be brave and determined, and while this is synonymous with acts of courage regarding heroic feats, such as climbing a mountain or saving someone from disaster, there are other ways it can manifest too. Indeed, if we reflect on the Lion from the film *The Wizard of Oz*, his journey to find courage saw him battling his fears: he feared his own shadow, although really it was standing in his power that he feared more. He eventually found his lionheart helped by his friends, since none of us are entirely alone on our own "yellow brick road." The person who succeeds and pushes through his panic, shaking inside and feeling vulnerable, is just as worthy of the "top" prize as the one who appears to master life more easily. Indeed, we often put others on pedestals, thinking they have superhuman powers, but this is an illusion, since everyone fights some internal battle; with what one finds easy, another finds difficult. We hold all emotions within us and have similar qualities and capabilities; they just need to be drawn out and used. Indeed, Jesus is known as both the Lamb of God, showing a meek and gentle persona, and the Lion of Judea, showing power and authority.

Today, notice any fear or uncertainty within you; do not judge whatever state you find yourself in but know that you also hold a lion's roar and heart that can be tapped into when needed. Sometimes we are scared to stand out, but if we look at the lion in nature, they are kings of the jungle; they intrinsically know their own majesty and symbolically are often linked to the energy of the sun, the lighthouse of our whole planet. They can be fierce, of course, and another famous lion, Aslan, from the book *The Lion, The Witch and The Wardrobe*, shows this clearly, the children being a little afraid at first but soon realizing his kind heart, goodness, and love. Aslan, like Christ, sacrifices himself for the greater good, and there is much relevant symbolism to Christ Consciousness within the stories. Another aspect linked to this card is that of the lioness in nature—an inspiring role model, one who looks after her family proudly and with determination, being both supreme protector and family (pride) member.

Learn to integrate the many positive qualities of the lion, since it will help you now. You may be at a time in your life when you are being asked to go it alone, personally, professionally, or in some other way. You may have lost a parent, have children who have left home, be starting a new business, or be entering a totally new chapter of your life. All require you to be strong, so lean on and remember other times when you have had to start anew, build from scratch, or venture into new terrain. Then you were able to accomplish more than you thought and were proud of what you achieved, and you will be again.

Lions are territorial, so protect and be proud of what you have earned: the people you love, the learning undertaken. You may also be moving to a new place or dwelling but know that like the lion, you can make any place your home and will be able to provide for yourself and others. A lion is self-reliant, independent, and a great survivor. Remember that if this is not how you currently see yourself, it IS what you are growing into. Be proud of how far you have already come, and alert to what lies ahead; with a lion's roar and heart, you will succeed.

KNIGHT'S VIGIL
PREPARE & GET READY

Knight's Vigil · PREPARE & GET READY

47

In days of old before being knighted, a squire (typically a nobleman) would spend time preparing himself in vigil; this would be an enforced period of no sleep (vigil comes from the Latin word *vigilia*, meaning wakefulness). He would cleanse his body, focus on prayer and his connection to God, and reflect on the moral and ethical code he would swear allegiance to. Vigils through the ages have also taken place before key events, religious ceremonies, and battles. At Gethsemane, Jesus spent time in prayer, alert to what was to come, knowing His battle would be physical, emotional, and spiritual. The crucifixion ahead would test Him to His limit, and He required time to gather His strength to be ready to face it, knowing it would also be His greatest triumph despite its challenge. When the disciples with Him fell asleep, He rebuked them, knowing how vital it was to prepare for the coming hours. Indeed, Jesus elsewhere readies them for their future respective missions, knowing He will not be physically around.

This is a key component to this card's message, to create time and space to prepare and align to God for the next stage to come. This doesn't mean it is a time of foreboding; simply that you are asked to give your best, be present, and be aware of your conduct and the impact you can make.

Living by a code that is resonant to your beliefs is highlighted right now, to stand for something, to align to a belief, to aspire to live your life by higher ideals that you set, and also to hold yourself accountable. Many of the qualities that knights of old held dear—nobility, grace, loyalty, courage, honor, integrity, humility, humbleness, and faithfulness—are ones that our world sorely needs modeled again. You are invited to hold them dear to your heart, inspiring others who may have forgotten that they are even important. You can do so even if the same respect is not shown to you. In a world where many are selfish, vain, and egocentric, living by a selfless, heart-centered code is empowering and divinely supported.

You are also encouraged to stand firm and be true to who you are, sovereign and free, not swayed by changing trends and fashions. You may be misunderstood and feel alone yet draw to you a band of like-minded brothers and sisters, such as King Arthur did with his twelve knights of the Round Table, and Christ did with His 12 apostles. Belonging to something, sharing a common belief, and remaining steadfast to a vision is important. New friendships and alliances may soon arrive, as well as a parting of the ways with those not willing to walk with you any further.

Change is here, and focus, determination, and a willingness to serve are highlighted. You will be guided by God and your higher self, and it is often said that when the student is ready, the Teacher appears, and this is such a time, learning new skills and expanding your knowledge.

Let go of any part of you that feels incapable, unworthy, or not up to the task. Everyone has flaws, yet the path of the knight is toward self-development, knowing from failure that strength and wisdom come, just as much as via victory and fortitude. Sink into quiet vigil, meditation, and prayer and gather your thoughts, collecting back scattered parts of yourself and becoming whole and centered. Your life and how you conduct it matters, and you are deeply appreciated and loved. Be at peace with all that is to come; you will conquer all that is ahead.

48

SPIRITUAL
PRACTICE
STRUCTURE & ROUTINE

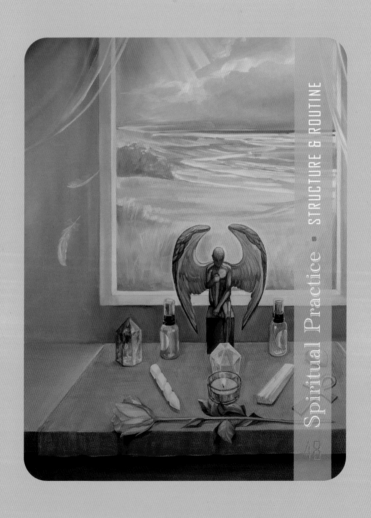

You are reminded of the importance of taking time to pause and connect with your higher self and your core beliefs, a time to sort through mental clutter and noise and come back to a state of inner peace. Without a regular spiritual practice, life becomes more frantic, unfocused, and harder than it needs to be. Spending time in quiet contemplation, joyous singing, chanting, or prayer all are recommended. It can be done alone or with others, but regularity and adding structure to your routine will bring maximum benefits of well-being. Without spiritual focus and a practice to support it, we can quickly lose our direction and become distracted and out of harmony, forgetting our true nature as a child of God. It also can be a way to nourish ourselves, filling up our own cup so we can serve others better, having received what we needed first. A spiritual practice also helps us reaffirm daily what we believe, and helps in our commitment to living a sacred life. It assists us on hard days when we seek help and during happier times too.

Think about what you currently do to connect, offer thanks, ask for guidance, or listen to spirit. It may be that this is a call to continuation of those actions or a suggestion to adapt or start something new. Sometimes we can say prayers on "automatic pilot," reciting well-known words without much conviction, but to be conscious of every word we utter or think takes prayer into a different level of communication. Meditation is also best done not squeezed into an expectation of what you want or think it should be, but rather a gradual unfolding of what it could be, which will change and flow accordingly. Having the space to listen and to be open to what arises is one of the greatest gifts you can give yourself. We surrender our will into thy will and become at one with the greater universe and God.

Anything done with intention is highlighted today; it could be via lighting a candle to remember a loved one, painting a mandala, doing a good deed to help another, observing silence, taking a mindful walk where every sense is alive to what wishes to be shown, or taking time to count your blessings and thank God for all you have. You may find it helpful to use tools to help still your mind, deepening your practice; these may include crystals, aromatherapy oils, prayer books, healing tinctures, incense, and more.

Setting up an altar in your home or workplace can also help create a conducive environment; fill this with meaningful things that help you connect—photographs, artwork, statues—these things simply act as "keys" to help bring you into deeper awareness, offering your senses cues that are helpful. Churches and places of worship have always been adorned with beauty; it is a way to celebrate God, but here no middleman is needed, and you create a direct and meaningful connection that enriches you deeply.

You are also reminded that spiritual practice is about how we conduct ourselves and how we live our life. To make our life a living testament to what we hold true and to honor it is the biggest way we can demonstrate our practice every day. To live as Jesus would.

49

PEACE
CALM CENTER, CALM MIND

There are many ways we can be triggered, angered, and made to feel unsettled, all of which profoundly impact our body and can result in us making poor decisions and choosing rashly from a place of panic or confusion rather than considered judgment and balance. Peace is so needed in our world and in our own lives and is made possible when we pause, breathe, and recenter, clearing our thoughts and aligning to our best selves.

In many ways the art of stone balancing demonstrates this well: being able to stand tall, balancing different things, reaching up to a single point of focus, and defying the laws of nature or reason by staying strong despite wild waters and winds trying to destabilize its structure.

To be the peace in the eye of the storm while others bicker or fight, to stay aligned when it is hardest—this is the goal we strive for and when it matters the most.

Peace doesn't have to be elusive or achievable only when conditions are "right"; it can be found in the middle of a storm and is an inner state gained via setting intention to be so by way of peaceful acts, calming words, and calm posture, breath, and manner. In every moment we have a choice regarding how we respond to anything; do we choose peace or do we choose a version of war? Will we enrage, inflame, or irritate often by being in ego, seeking confrontation, belittlement, or argument? Or will we be in peace and come from our heart, offering something softer?

Look at situations that may not be in harmony, and ask what I can do to help bring peace today. It may be a small or big gesture, action, or thought, but it starts as a seed and grows from there.

Jesus said, "Peace be with you and peace I leave you," demonstrating the importance of both holding and spreading peace wherever we go. He encourages us to leave a legacy and be remembered as a peacemaker, where we helped build bridges, brought different parties together, and created harmony in our families, communities, and wider world.

To "come in peace" is also highlighted, to set our intentions that we seek calm waters and that we arrive with no hidden agenda or manipulated intent. Much of this is about being crystal clear in our dealings with people, "who you see is who you get," and being consistent in nature and willing to apologize when we go astray.

To hold peace, it is important to be observant and mindful of your own reactions, to acknowledge your feelings and be true to them. Very few of us can hold peaceful thoughts always, so we should not be too self-critical but instead notice our imbalance and then self-correct ourselves to restore harmony and peace within.

Ask what you can do today that is going to help bring inner peace. It may be an activity to calm the mind and allow stillness, via mindfulness meditation, quiet music, gardening, baking, being with calm friends, walking, or any activity we love. To "chop wood and carry water" reminds us too that how we navigate our daily routines can also be a tool to harmony, via doing one thing mindfully rather than scattering our energy and rushing through our day.

Affirming I am Peace, I bring peace, and I wish you peace to others and ourselves serves you today and is found within the heart, which carries its energy always.

SACRED SEXUALITY
HEALING & CONNECTION

Sacred Sexuality · HEALING & CONNECTION

50

You may feel as though sacred sexuality is something that has passed you by, has been lost, or is an unobtainable goal. And yet, there is rich teaching within this message, whether you have experienced it or not, are already holding its vibration, or are in partnership or single. Sacred sexuality is less a practice (although tantric techniques and philosophy are one avenue) and more a far-wider unique path, and however you approach it, it is ultimately about deepening connection to yourself, another, and God. Many belief systems have at their core the holy sanctity of sex, some decreeing that sex only within marriage is acceptable. However, it is important to realize that Jesus's narrow words on this were written decades after His teaching and were led by current thinking of the day and the writers themselves. If you ask Jesus now, His teaching is that sacred sexuality is to be celebrated, not condemned; the body is what God has given, and divine connection is to be cherished, not be laden with judgment and rules.

Indeed, any relationship Jesus had when alive as a man is not in the Gospels, but that is not to say He had to be celibate, because God created everything, including our ability to procreate but also to receive pleasure. Indeed, when we look at enforced celibacy (as opposed to celibacy we choose), it can lead to unneeded hardship, and in New Earth consciousness we are not forced to take such vows of abstinence if we do not want to. Back to Adam and Eve at the tree, woman is no longer "cast out" and condemned for her actions of temptation but is instead recognized as the abundant goddess she is. Now we are all invited back into Eden, where mutual respect, appreciation, balance, harmony, and love are the only prerequisites.

Because you are, if you're an adult, a sexual being with a body that has needs, the question asked is whether these are met by a suitor with energy aligned to yours and seeking ultimate expression of love. It may also be worth considering if you are a good partner, able to give as well as receive and be vulnerable while seeking deeper intimacy and mutual goals. If the energy between you is overtly influenced by mass media, marketing, and the entertainment industry, there may be a distorted expectation and disillusionment with our physical appearance via unrealistic airbrushed imagery or toxic material viewed.

Sacred sexuality is about being open to the far-deeper emotional and spiritual aspects of embracing and enjoying an intimate life. Nowadays the fast pace of life can be matched with the hunt for quick gain, whether through one-off encounters or relationships that don't get time to reveal what they can ultimately be. The rush toward being with someone because it is expected, or you feel pressured by your peers, can lead to problems also. Instead, like waiting for the sun to rise, some things are worth waiting for and some unions are destined.

Letting go of old dogma, shame, guilt, apprehension, or feeling undesirable is necessary, since your body is not something to be embarrassed or ashamed of; it may be that healing from past abuse or dysfunctional and unwanted experiences may be needed. If required, enter the holy waters so you can begin anew, ready to welcome in new possibilities, experiences, vulnerability, sharing, and love. Tenderness, openheartedness, excitement, bliss, ecstasy, and new states of consciousness arrive, reminding you of the feeling of being alive.

51

ABUNDANCE

ENJOY LIFE FULLY

The path to enlightenment via Christ Consciousness is not about suffering, pain, or living in fear of a spiteful God out to gain vengeance and retribution. Neither is it about having guilt for what we have or shame for enjoying ourselves. Far from it; living this way is instead about opening to the abundance and goodness of this beautiful planet and life, its rich resources, places to visit, things to see and do, and people to help.

Even when we go through hard times, there will be those who step up to extend the hand of friendship or offer support in another way. The meal cooked, the children looked after, the kind and unexpected gesture, or simply a stranger's smile that is directed toward you on a gloomy day. Our animal friends can provide much companionship, affection, and healing, too, showering us with unconditional love and teaching us much. These are all examples of abundance, and yet we often fail to acknowledge them as such.

Taking time to stop and appreciate all that is precious helps us remember how much we have, and that God has given us, the birds in the sky, the fish in the sea, the animals, trees bearing fruit, night and day, and of course each other. At each point of creation, we are told God said, "It was good," and this life—which by nature is short—is meant to be enjoyed and savored; it is not a trial or meant to be an ordeal.

So much of how we respond to life is via our attitude and inner belief system. Ask yourself today if you are expecting and anticipating good fortune, abundance, and joy, or if you are worried waiting for the next thing to go wrong or be taken away. Many of us have been hurt or betrayed by circumstances in life, but we must not let it taint our projections of what the rest of our time here will be like.

How we perceive life is how it is, and what seeds we throw into the future is up to us to choose and sow wisely. Are we dwelling on failure, danger, obstacles, and lack or are we focusing on what we still have, knowing more will be provided? The farmer (who is each one of us) must have faith in the "crop" and water it well with good deeds, charity, kindness, thanks, and love. In God's playground we have been given all we need; it is ours for the taking as long as we share and help each other along.

Jesus also was present at various feasts and happy gatherings; in Cana he turned the water into wine for the wedding guests, and this is as far from old vows of denial and abstinence as we can get. It is OK to have fun, enjoy company, laugh, sing, enjoy good food, and celebrate all we have been given, including each other.

Think about what an abundant life means to you. It may involve free time, family, travel, a nice house, living a full and varied life or a far simpler one; even a monastic life is fine if it makes you happy. Take time today to stop and smell the flowers, be with someone you love, appreciate friends, laugh, and be entertained. To feel the breeze in your hair, taste the meal at the end of the day, and find comfort from the warm bed at night. There is also a message here to balance work and play, to take time off to recharge and relax, to plan a trip or night out, to treat yourself to something nice, or to pamper yourself and put your feet up. To live an abundant life is what we all truly deserve, and what is obtainable too.

52

SONG

CELEBRATE & EXPRESS YOURSELF

Open your ears to hear God's voice all around you, from the children's chatter on the school bus to the rain on the window, the cat's purr, a favorite band, and a baby's laughter. The world is full of sound and melody, and we grew up with many types, from hymns to gospel renditions, psalms, and choral wonders to the chanting of Buddhist monks and the drumbeat of Indigenous cultures. Song is a way of uniting us and a way to honor traditions, our history, and our culture, as well as birthing new paradigms and expressing a time. As we move into the golden age, music can help walk us there with new frequencies, vibrations, symphonies, and more. Music's purpose is to raise our vibration, helping us express our feelings and mood, and in holy practice lifting reverence to heaven as a gift of thanks for all that we have.

Today the inclusion of song and music will lift your soul, raise a smile, help your feet move, and help your tears fall, whether in sadness, joy, or any other emotion. Just as the parent soothes the child with a lullaby, you too can soothe yourself via the power of song, which can transport you back to happier bygone times and nourish and replenish you as good memories do.

You were given a voice to use, so be proud of it, sing, hum, since the timbre of your voice, the unique way it sounds, your accent, and how you string words together are beautiful to God, who loves to hear it.

The sounds of melodies, drumbeats, percussion, gentle bells, and the piano's majestic chords all enrich our time here on Earth. Taking up an instrument also can be fun and educational at this time, birthing new languages made up of chords, notes, and quavers . . . stimulating our minds and moving us into new talents, hobbies, or even a career. Everyone can learn, since rhythm is in-built within you; you don't need a qualification to pick up a drum or strum a guitar, so have fun learning and explore your connection to music, as well as moving your body to its beat and rhythm. Music has weaved itself through all of time and was cherished and honored in ancient cultures as well as now—to help heal, celebrate, mourn, ward off bad energies, and mark the seasons and cycles of life.

When was the last time you sang or listened to a piece of music that stirred your soul and shifted the energy within you to be inspired and move? Today, listen to what you enjoy, participate, and notice the creation of sound, from wind chimes at the window, to humming a tune in the shower, to the clatter of pots and pans in the kitchen and the noise of a household waking up and going about the day.

Music can bring happiness into an empty room, be company if alone, change mood, contribute to the party or gathering, and create ambiance and atmosphere to lift frequency and bring you closer to God. Enjoy all expressions and manifestations of it; this may be a time to go and hear live music, book tickets to the opera, sit in a bar with a live jazz band, or hear the percussion band playing as they march. The sounds of the universe are beautiful to behold, and one of God's gifts to us; enjoy exploring all forms today.

53

HOLY ANGER
BE THE CHANGE

Holy Anger · BE THE CHANGE

53

Do you believe in fully living your life, seeing each day as a gift and precious beyond measure? This may seem an odd question for a card about resurrection, since death is the factor preceding it, yet we can unconsciously operate and live as if we are already "half dead," either willing the years to go faster (as a consequence of grief or unhealed trauma), waiting for something to happen first ("then my life will really begin"), or be on automatic pilot, going through the motions with no awareness or presence.

We can also fear death, scared of what is to come and not understanding that death is a natural part of nature's cycle, and there can be nothing new without it! Fear denies the wonder of God's creation in all its forms and stops us from stepping into our dreams and welcoming new experiences, events, and people. We become reclusive, not wanting to venture into our fullest expression and journey while here, full of doubt, consequently thwarting growth, and ending up living a lesser life—in many ways we are more afraid to LIVE than to die.

In the story of Lazarus, where Jesus raises a dead man from a tomb, it is interesting that the disciples first interpret that the man is simply sleeping, not dead. Although Jesus later confirms he had indeed died, the ambiguity of both sleep and death itself within the same passage is noteworthy. Actual death is merely stepping forward into another realm of existence, but we can waste time and sleepwalk through life, not caring to explore the meaning of life or the mysteries of creation and faith. However, walking in Christ Consciousness is a chosen path by those who seek to grow, learn, and evolve, and asks us not just to celebrate our eternal life, but to enjoy the life we have now, to make the most of every day, a blessing despite anything going on around us. Being alive and allowing the soul's growth through every chapter, joyous and sad, is why we chose to incarnate, and why we will likely do so again.

Jesus said, "I am the Resurrection and the Life; he who believes in me will not die," a clear teaching on the continuation of life and that via embodying the qualities of love, grace, and all that He taught, the turning of the wheels between different planes of existence would be ensured. Knowing this gives us a bedrock of security, which can encourage us to want to do more, not wanting to waste a single moment, knowing we are always held.

Rebirth and resurrection occur every day upon waking; we have a chance to start over, try again, and embrace what we can create. To turn challenges into triumph, and sadness into reflection and eventually laughter, and to see how every part fits to bring about the tapestry of our lives.

Today, sit and feel into what you are ready to let go of and what parts of your life are complete, giving thanks to all you learned. Pause, breathe, and take a moment to welcome in new energies that can transform and elevate your world, aspiring to live a full life, made up of myriad moments. Know that your rebirth and resurrection are here, and a new chapter waits for you to enter its pages. Have no fear; step into it fully, and as the stone rolls back from the tomb of where you have been, you feel the sunlight on your face.

Love is here, New Life is here, God is here within you, and you are free.

Conclusion

To conclude, I very much hope that this deck has both given you food for thought and reignited the Christ Consciousness energy within you. For me, having been around the stories of Jesus my whole life, writing this book rekindled my own love for Him and helped me honor the light more deeply He encourages us to carry within ourselves. Doing so has made me appreciate through fresh eyes the beautiful teachings He gave and encouraged us to model. Falling back in love with these tenants of heart-centered living, I recognize even more their value as the foundation blocks in my own life. I hope that this deck will inspire you and help you live a peaceful and content life, safe in the knowledge that you are divinely loved and always supported. My wish is that the guidance on navigating the challenging parts of your journey found within this work is helpful and meaningful, and that it focuses your attention every day on self-development and your spiritual path.

While around us, we all see so much that is difficult in our world, and behaviors that are the opposite of a loving response. Recognize and remember the immense importance and contribution you make in helping the world by choosing love.

Love—the most powerful energy in this world—it heals, unifies, breaks down barriers, and brings us back to our true sentient nature. Thank you for choosing this deck and for all you do to make this world a better place.

About the Author

AMANDA ELLIS is a spiritual teacher, writer, and healer. As a channel to the Higher Realms, she has as her two main guides Jesus and Archangel Metatron. She is widely known also for her work with the angels and other Ascended Masters and is a fully qualified and experienced color therapist. She is the creator of a system of healing called Metatron Color Healing™, provides online training, and is also the creator of a range of handmade powerful aura sprays that are distributed widely around the world. She is an internationally recognized expert in her field and has a wide client base, offering guidance  across various online platforms. She also runs workshops and events and is a proficient public speaker.

Amanda is the author of *The Archangel Metatron Self-Mastery Oracle*. She lives on the South Coast of England beside the sea with her two daughters and husband, close to the ley lines connecting to Stonehenge, Avebury, and Glastonbury.

To find out more about Amanda and her work, visit www.angeliccelestialcolours.co.uk or You Tube at Amanda Ellis.

About the Artist

JANE DELAFORD TAYLOR is a professional artist and illustrator, well known for her inspirational paintings, which seek to capture the energy and light of the angelic realm. Jane is also a trained healer, having studied homeopathy, Reiki, and emotional freedom techniques (EFT) to practitioner level, and she believes visual art is an important channel that can be used for healing and change on many levels, since it speaks to our subconscious mind and engages directly with the soul.

"This process also affects the artist, of course, and working closely with Amanda during the creation of this card deck was both challenging and enlightening for me. The many hours of consulting, meditating, and painting were made enjoyable by the way this project just seemed to flow as if we had a Divine Art Director on the team, which of course we did! I trust that everyone who uses the deck will find that same divine flow entering their own lives, along with the wisdom in the words."

Jane works from her cottage studio in Scotland, beside the Holy Loch. You can see more of her work at www.janedelafordtaylor.com.